Becoming Dynamic

Stories of Women Rising to Greatness Despite Their Circumstances

An Anthology
Edited By Dr. Denise Nicholson

Foreword by Lisa Nichols

Dedication

This book is dedicated to all who are struggling to make sense of life. To all who feel the pressure of just being alive. All the things you are experiencing and all the things you have experienced will work for your good. Don't be ashamed or afraid to STAND on your story. You have the power to **Become Dynamic.**

Acknowledgements

Thank you to all the women who came together to lend their incredibly emotionally-honest stories to make this book so meaningful and impactful. Thanks to the editors whose commitment to excellence helped to produce a book we all can be proud of.

Special thanks to editor Sonia Brown for her attention to the intricate details that make all the difference in such an important project with so many moving parts.

To my mentor Mr. Les Brown for working with me to create the perfect title; you are awesome.

Thank you, Toni Jones, for all the lessons you have taught me and all the contributing authors of this anthology through your music. Your music is a constant reminder that we are worthy, and your message of empowerment has boosted our confidence and caused a positive shift in our lives. We are honored to have your contribution to this book.

To Lisa Nichols, who opened up my world and that of many others to the joys of healing and transformation, thank you.

Foreword

by Lisa Nichols

We've always heard stories of the grandmother's resilience; the stories of walking miles to school, cooking dinner in an outdoor fire space, or making a small amount of currency go a very long way. I have the pleasure to inform you that there are modern-day "sheroes" like that, who are walking amongst us every day—women like you and me who choose each day to rise above our circumstances.

We may have had times when we became entangled under our circumstances. Alternatively, we may have felt the magnificence of standing on a mountaintop that we spent years climbing. We may have also felt the weight of being crushed by our own chaos, or by a dream that didn't pan out the way we intended. Maybe we are nursing the wound of a love that didn't manifest the way we imagined, or we are seeing the nightfall once more upon some deep-seated distress.

You see, some of us may have freshly inherited pain, with no idea of how to combat this soul-shaking violence that crept up in our space and left us with deep silence, or left us emotionally inflamed. We have danced to the best rhythms, and we have fallen hard on the sharpest floor. Whatever our situations and whatever spaces we may have found ourselves jammed in, we are dynamic women.

Dynamic women come in every complexion and every nationality. We fall under every religious sector, every spiritual realm from every socio-economic background. Often, we fail to realize just how dynamic we are because we are so busy fighting the demons of doubt and imposter syndrome. We are often slaying the dragons of financial obligations, while supporting families, community activism, and social needs. Seldomly do we look down to even see the "S" on our chests or recognize that the "S" can peel off. We don't realize that the cape has 'velcro' on it, and that we can set them both aside and catch our breath with other "supersheroes"—other dynamic women like ourselves.

I founded the Dynamic Women's Organization, which is not formalized, nor incorporated—just shaped by desire. I also founded this delicious experience called, The Dynamic Women's Retreat, because I needed a safe space to catch my breath, take my cape off and sew up the holes in my cape to let the "S" on my chest take a rest.

I needed a place to re-choose Lisa, to reignite my soul, to rejuvenate my spirit, and to reactivate my dreams. I needed a place where I could forgive myself and cry the un-cried tears. I needed a safe space to give myself permission to be as wildly successful as I am now. I needed to give myself permission to embrace all of the things that brought me to the very first day I stepped into the Dynamic Women's Space in Barcelona, so that I could give myself permission to receive everything that was on its way to me.

Initially, the Dynamic Women's Retreat was quite selfishly something that I needed. I was not aware that so many other women needed it. However, there showed up other women like me, who were like-minded, equally ambitious, and equally desiring of a safe space. I was shocked that many super-sister soldiers were saying, "I can 'Wakanda' during the day, but can I have a safe place to lay my head at night, and not just next to a love interest? I want a sisterhood."

You see, I had met women after women who wanted a sisterhood but had been violated, betrayed, or abandoned at some point in their lives by another sister. Therefore, they questioned whether they could ever trust women again. I believe that no one can hold a black woman in her darkest hours quite like another black woman; no one can empathize with a black woman like another black woman.

That is not to discount anybody else, but I'm saying, *a sister knows how to hold a sister and put herself in the other sister's shoes.* A sister knows how to stand in front of a sister and be her bodyguard, her armor, and her accountability. Surprise hashtag? Not so surprised. Other dynamic women needed it as well.

The Dynamic Women Organization is a sacred group of global leaders, families, and "supersheroes" disguised as everyday women. It is a sacred organization that most dynamic women do not even know that they belong to. It is a place for everyday modern-day "sheroes"; women like you and me who choose each day to rise above our circumstances.

The purpose of the dynamic women's retreat was to rest, re-choose, rejuvenate, press reset, or reignite fires, and shine a light on women like us, who go unmentioned. For the most part they are being—strong, brave, overcoming, and *Becoming Dynamic.*

You may have had the glory and the pleasure of being at one of our sacred retreats, where we laugh hard, cry deep, dance long and strong, and eat heartily. You may not have had the pleasure of experiencing one of our retreats, but as you are now reading this book you will feel the connection to the words, to a story that reminds you of your chaos, or one that reminds you of your brilliance or your magnificence. You are a dynamic woman and I salute you!

As you read this book, may you wake up to the dawn of a new day filled with hope, and a new meaning of who you are despite your circumstances. Whenever you come to a dynamic retreat, your other sisters and I will say, "Welcome home."

Lisa Nichols is one of the world's most-requested motivational speakers, as well as a media personality and corporate CEO whose global platform has reached nearly 80 million people. From a struggling single mom on public assistance to a millionaire entrepreneur, Lisa's courage and determination has inspired fans worldwide and helped countless audiences "breakthrough", to discover their own untapped talents and infinite potential.

As Founder and Chief Executive Officer of Motivating the Masses, Inc., Lisa has developed workshops and programs that have transformed the lives of countless men and women, and altered the trajectory of businesses throughout the country and across the world.

Lisa is also a best-selling author of six books, and her 7th book ABUNDANCE NOW, was published in 2016 by HarperCollins. In ABUNDANCE NOW, Lisa continues her journey with her fans, providing a clear and practical blueprint for personal success, drawn directly from the life experiences of its beloved author. ABUNDANCE NOW is the follow-up to Lisa's New York Times Best Seller, NO MATTER WHAT.

To contact Lisa, please see below:

Email: support@motivatingthemasses.com

Contents

Preface

By Toni Jones

I grew up wanting to be like Jesus; not just believing in Jesus. I thought healing the sick, raising the dead, turning water into wine, and walking on water was the coolest thing ever. I couldn't believe that no one around me wanted to learn how to do these miracles. I did research and sought guidance to help me fulfill my desire for miracle working, but to no avail. I felt that no one understood my yearning for the supernatural.

One day while reading the Good Book (the Bible) I came across this scripture, "On these two laws hang the whole Law of God, if you do this you fulfill the Law of God: Love God with your heart, mind and soul and love your neighbor as you love yourself." It was then that my mind opened up and I said to myself, "If I can't walk on water and do all these miraculous things, I'll learn how to love, since this would be like killing a thousand birds with one stone." So, this is where my healing journey began; I didn't even know what I was signing up for.

Throughout my journey of self-discovery, trying my best to navigate my conditioning and programming, I always prayed, "God keep my heart pure." It terrified me to think that heartbreak, pain, trauma and life circumstances could change me. At one particular point in time I looked over my past ten years and realized that all I had been doing was trying to make relationships with men work. That's what I was doing with my life for years. My attention was always occupied by the sidetracks of wanting to be chosen by a man. I was horrified! I needed something to restore my pride and dignity. So, I went back to school to get my degree in Psychology; and little did I know, it was a portal into enlightenment of the self.

The more I learned the more obsessed I became about the human *makeup*, and who I really was. I then tried figuring out how to create my true self. That's what led me to Lisa Nichols. I've heard from so many gurus, thought leaders, philosophers, and spiritualists but seeing and hearing Lisa speak, feeling her expression of deep simple truths; to see a Melanated Free woman in mind, heart, and soul was revolutionary for me. I knew I wanted my liberation, my own inner freedom; and she was a representation of that possibility. Choice by choice, pain after pain, lesson after lesson throughout all the seasonal changes that occurred in my life, I learned to choose my freedom over everything. I didn't want to be held hostage to my inner demons, traumatizing memories and generational curses any more.

Lisa represented more than a teacher to me. She was, and is, a representation of what I believed to be my liberator: that one who could make it possible for me to speak to the masses, to champion my melanated sisters with healing, consciousness, and most importantly PURE LOVE—by just being myself. So, do you see that my path required Lisa Nichols? It required her experiences of painful growth decisions and her lonely seasons. Her shadows were necessary for my path. She had to remember, she had to heal, she had to transcend temporary narratives, because I, and so many others, were waiting for her story, her brilliance, her testimony, her triumphs, her lessons, her essence, and her love.

I knew I had to meet this woman. I had a core group of six women who were helping me, to raise me—she was one of them. At the time I had a friend that worked in youth advocacy who knew I loved Lisa. She told me we were invited to a youth retreat and that Lisa was going to be there—we would be camping out with her. We traveled into the mountains which was pretty scary, and after hours of traveling we got there, only to find out that she couldn't make it. I was so disappointed because so much went into making it there; however in the event I then got called upon to minister to the youth. I spoke to them with all my heart because I knew they were just like me, having no guidance into who they truly were.

Even though I didn't get the chance to meet Lisa in person, I know that I will eventually. I mean, look,

I am writing a dedication in a book dedicated to her. Remember that initially I had this notion that I was born to be working and experiencing miracles. I didn't know that my freedom was the path to miracles. Lisa showed and taught me that and for the first time I saw the clear vision of reaching millions of people. I would begin by touching my sisters first and from there the message would spread to the masses—the human family. I saw loving myself as a cure for more than I can think of. Lisa was the living "billboard" to my awakening, healing, and inner consciousness to the fact that I am the miracle.

I will one day meet her and we will hug and do that rocking side to side that we melanated gals do with celebration and glee: exchanging words that are felt and not heard, because we are living miracles, performing miracles. We are free! We know that we are loved, and we are LOVE. I am honored to write this dedicated foreword to acknowledge and celebrate Lisa Nichols for using her voice, her offerings, and the time she invests in her community. I am what I am today because of who you are, Lisa; and I thank you with deep gratitude, for raising a woman like me.

Toni Jones, is an *Affirmation Musician* who found creative ways to promote the message of conscious well-being and mental health. She hopes to inspire women to become more conscious about their well-being in a culture that drowns women's entrepreneurship and empowerment with workaholism. One way that she creates to promote this message is through music.

Through her affirmation albums; "Affirmations for The Grown Ass Woman", "Affirmations and Chill", "I see Me Mantras", "Getcha Mind Right" and her newly released album on 11.11.21 "ME -VS- EVERYME Affirmations of Self Love", she is spreading the message of her brand, to "Wife Your Life" through well-being, throughout the world. She has surpassed **10 million streams** and is growing.

Website: https://solo.to/iamtonijones

Email: booking-management@iamsounds.com

Introduction

By Dr. Denise Nicholson

I was a fifteen-year-old girl when told, "If you don't have an abortion, you can't stay in this house." I left my aunt's house that night and went to live with my boyfriend and his family. When the morning broke, I woke up being a woman, and the struggles of life for most women that looked like me ensued. Life was tough: therefore, I have never thought of myself as a dynamic woman. Have you ever thought of yourself as being dynamic? How does one become dynamic? To become dynamic, **you have to work on yourself.** Look at your current situation and see the changes you need to make. Then make a list of all the changes you would like despite your circumstances. Make a plan to achieve those things and make learning a part of your daily life. No matter what, stick to the plan. After a few years, you will wake up and realize that you are living your dreams—becoming dynamic.

I was a teenage mother, so according to society, I was more of a statistic than I was dynamic—especially in my early years. I finished high school and then heard of an opportunity to become a hairstylist, so I signed up for beauty school. That inspired a desire in my heart to own my own business and that is how I became an entrepreneur. A few years later, I went back to school and became a registered nurse.

In the Fall of 2004, I was diagnosed with depression and started listening to motivational speakers to help inspire me through my rough days. I then started working on myself. I became a nurse practitioner and further went on to become a Doctor of Nursing Practice, yet, I didn't feel there was anything dynamic about my story.

A few years after being diagnosed with depression, I wrote a book about the pain I felt as an orphaned child, and the pain I felt while growing up and becoming a woman. Other women shared similar stories of their pains with me, and I included their stories; that's how the book, ***Se-lah: When Mommy Left for Farin*** was born. My book became a bestseller and garnered a lot of attention. People from the Jamaican, Caribbean, and African diaspora wanted to interview me, and that is how I started getting speaking engagements. At those speaking engagements, many individuals had questions concerning how they could write a book. That is what gave birth to the great idea, to start a book writing class.

I happened to pounce upon Lisa Nichols on the internet while learning how to speak for impact. Lisa

Nichols was one of the teachers who taught me how to speak effectively and how to "Speak for Profit." I have been coached by her (not privately) ever since, on many aspects of my life.

Everything about Lisa resonated with me. She was a black woman who had struggles just like me, yet she was thriving. Her single mother story was inspiring, but her tenacity to save money consistently helped me to create a saving plan of my own. Her story of triumph over difficult times in her life motivated and inspired me. I was greatly encouraged by her life experience.

When a book-writing client who turned friend told me she was going to a Dynamic Women's Retreat, I wanted to attend also; not because I thought I was dynamic, but because Lisa was going to be there. She was the woman who had overcome it all and had taught me how to "Speak for Profit". Lisa changed my life.

Thirty-six other black women from all over the world were at this Dynamic Women's Retreat, looking to work on themselves and help others heal. These women had achieved much success and yet were still not feeling complete. Although I didn't think that I belonged there initially, after hearing the women's stories, I realized that we were all on the same journey, looking for the next step or the next feat that would help us to become whole or healed. We were all accomplished women, working on ourselves.

We were encouraged to get to know each other through different exercises. I learned a lot about these women in the room. There were lawyers, doctors, physicians, preachers, teachers, soldiers of every rank, CEOs, and life coaches; you name it, they were there with one common theme—Black women seeking wholeness.

It was beautiful to see so many high-achieving women in the same room, and it was more encouraging to me because they all reminded me of myself—black women who, despite their circumstances, have triumphed!

Black women are often looked at as strong caregivers who carry the weight of others' burdens yet do not share their issues. In this anthology, the women have left their "supershero" capes behind, as my coach Lisa Nichols would say, and have shared their authentic truth. You will find many different incredible moving stories of women: their traumas, their disappointments, and the pain or the struggles they overcame to find themselves.

In addition, you will find expressive and uplifting poetry, as each woman chooses how to express her authentic self. Each of these stories or poems is unique and stimulating as they engage the readers.

By the end of reading this anthology, my hope is for you to find a powerful message that will resonate with you even after you have finished the stories.

I hope you, the reader, are encouraged to work on yourself, not because something is wrong with you, but because self-improvement is a necessary life-long process that we all need to fulfill our lives, to be healed and to be made whole.

Self-improvement involves a growth mindset, learning new things, and discovering more about ourselves and what we are capable of. It is the unfolding of different areas of our lives that make us unique, special, and dynamic.

We are all subject to unavoidable problems, irreversible consequences, predictable lives, and some very unpredictable tragedies. My recommendation to you, dear reader, is to focus on your strengths no matter your circumstances. Declutter your life and give yourself room to grow. Ask yourself powerful questions about who you are and who you would like to become. Seek feedback from like-minded individuals. Work with an accountability partner to ensure that you reach new goals. Dream big but start with small goals. Each win will give you the confidence to move on to the next win. Keep moving forward no matter what and develop a stick-to-itiveness about you. Commit to curiosity, for learning is ongoing. Take daily actions towards your goal and when you get results, celebrate your successes.

This book is yet another space where "supersheroes" leave their "capes" behind and share their experiences of rising to greatness, despite their circumstances.

You will be able to relate to the stories, reflect on them and then reflect on your own life. Each of these short stories or poems is thought-provoking. As the authors share their vulnerability, you will be immersed in their stories, experiencing their challenges and triumphs.

So, am I a dynamic woman? Are you a dynamic woman? Indeed! Lisa Nichols says I am, and I'm sure she'll say the same about you. A dynamic woman focuses on who she is: the core of what makes her the woman she has become, not her titles or lack thereof. It is not what she does, but what she has overcome. She is dynamic when she does her best with what she has, and when she reaches inward for more growth and healing. She is dynamic when she has excavated herself and accepted all of who she is—her authentic, dynamic self.

Lisa Nichols, thank you is not enough to say to you for the life-changing experiences, healings, breakthroughs, friendships, networking, and accountability that through your ministry were established at the Dynamic Women's Retreat. We women collaborated and combined this anthology as a token to you, from all the dynamic women around the world, whose lives you have impacted and changed. This book is to say we honor you and your dedication to serving women. We appreciate you, and we are grateful for your life and the passion you display in helping us to become dynamic women.

Dr. Denise Nicholson is an inspira-tional, insightful, and transformational speaker with the gift of telling stories. She is a native of Jamaica, West Indies and migrated to Mount Vernon, New York as a teenager. She became a teenage mother who then overcame many obstacles to become a successful entrepreneur.

She is a best-selling author and the founder of **Bold Publishing Company**: A publishing house that mentors and coaches speakers and leaders to get their book ideas out of their heads, put them on paper, become best-selling authors, and make revenue.

As a result of her mentoring program, hundreds of writers have become published authors and have developed courses to complement their books; earning them consistent six-figure incomes. If you or anyone you know have a dream of becoming an author, **Bold Publishing** can help. If you have any questions the contact information is below.

website: https://denisenicholson.com
Email: authordnicholson@gmail.com
Instagram: @authordenisenicholon

Chapter 1

*Moving From Victimhood to
Empowered Dynamic Woman*
By Terri Wade

I n the spring of 1996 when I was just eight years old, I knew I wanted to die; so, I planned how to end my life. You know the story of Cinderella: the two steps sisters and her evil stepmom—that was the story of my life as a young child. I was constantly bullied into doing the most demeaning chores and cleaning up around the house.

Most unfortunately, I had let their actions and opinions of me determine my self-worth... For example: I thought and believed that I didn't matter; that I wasn't lovable and that everyone would be better off if I wasn't around. Because of this mindset I punished myself for every mistake that I thought I made, confirming the belief: *you are so stupid.*

In fact, one of my most vivid memories was when "we" were told to clean the walk-in closet. We used it as a playroom, where we ate and played with the toys that our dad bought for us. Forgotten snacks over the months became rotten, and the bugs and maggots took over. It was I alone who had to sit in the middle of the playroom with the insects that had taken over; to clean it all up by myself.

At the time my mom was in rehab, and my dad worked for what seemed like all the time; so he could give my step mom, step sisters and I "the good life". Of course, he had good intentions and showed me love the way he knew how. I have since learned that through intense hours of personal development, my spiritual awakening, and doing the love language quiz. I learnt that my father's love languages were gifts and acts of service which he did well; and my love languages were quality time and touch which I was not getting. So, at that moment, sitting in that small room filled with maggots, I had had enough! *If this is life, I want nothing to do with it, was my thought*.

One day the opportunity presented itself. I remember walking down this narrow hallway in our home; on my way to the bathroom. I noticed through the small crack in my dad's room; that he was closing his dresser drawer, and just before he closed it, I saw a gun in it. My mind began to race. *That's it! This could be my way out of the painful bullying and being such a problem to everyone*, I thought.

I started to put together a plan: I knew my dad would be working when I got back from school. When my step sisters were not looking, I would go into his room, close the door behind me, open the drawer with the gun in it, put the gun up to my head and pull the trigger. Now that I had my plan together, I shared it with the one friend I had at that time, Jenny. And, as a good friend should do, she told her dad, who then told my dad. So, after school, I was picked up and was taken straight to therapy.

What happened in therapy saved my life! I had no clue that our thoughts create how we feel and ultimately how we perceive and experience the world. Subsequently, I kept feeling like the victim in my life story. I replayed the same thoughts as a young child that, *nobody wanted to play with me and that I was so stupid.* I learned that most people have 80% negative thoughts and replay the same 90% from the day before. The therapist listened to me, and she played games with me while giving me positive affirmations: that I was really good at the games, that I was very sweet, and so on. Those affirmations helped with feelings of self-worth for the first time in my young life. My self-esteem SLOWLY began to rise.

Soon after, my mom got out of rehab (yay!) and her best motherly advice to me was, "Fake it until you make it." So, I would put a smile on my face, though I was still very quiet. I noticed when I smiled, people would smile back, and I liked it a lot. I also liked and appreciated that they didn't ask me what was wrong when I wasn't smiling. Today, I've learned through getting certified in Positive Psychology Coaching, that smiling releases dopamine in our brains that chemically makes us happier. With my newfound confidence and happiness, I started excelling in gymnastics, making more friends and building up self-worth.

Fast forward today I now inspire thousands of people online, in courses and at in-person events. I am the Founder of the Lady Entrepreneur Society, a Positive Psychology Coach, A Course in Miracles Teacher, and an Intuitive Speaker. I run a mastermind that helps ladies confidently step into the very best version of themselves, connect to their truth, and make money doing just what my mother taught me. Except I don't feel that we need to fake it until we make it. We need to believe while we become it: believing in the unseen, and having faith that you can be, do, and have whatever you desire. Then, you must act as if you are already the person now who has the life, the confidence, the love, and the success that you desire; until it is embodied, knowing that you are that powerful, dynamic woman, and have had her in you all along.

Many of my clients feel like an imposter as they begin to step into the best version of themself, (I've been there!) And you're reading this may sometimes feel that way. The key is to know yourself, your true self: your true essence as a spirit being. We are spiritual beings having a human experience. We have been created by a loving Presence, made in the same image, with the same loving, joyful and creative capabilities. We are the creators, and it is so empowering when you grasp this truth.

I can feel confident in this truth as I deepen my spiritual awareness through meditation, studying, and remembering my time of revelation: "Revelation induces complete but temporary suspension of doubt and fear. It reflects the original form of communication between God and His creations." (ACIM, Chapter 1.II.1:1) It was the best moment I had ever experienced, and I know that it is our true state of being or what some call Heaven! I understand that we get to choose how we feel, the story we tell, and our perception. We can choose to come from a place of empowerment, strength, compassion, forgiveness, and love: to change the way we see things, and then things we see, will change.

My mission today is to help ladies change their mindset, to see things differently and not let their mind wander into what they don't want and to focus only on what they do want. In doing so they can experience the confidence, the happiness, the peace, the freedom, and the prosperity they deserve; to become dynamic women!

A dynamic woman knows herself, loves herself, trusts herself, believes in herself and honors herself. A dynamic woman heals herself in order to heal others and bring forth any of her desires. She moves despite the fear she may feel because she knows it is not actually real. Fear is an illusion; it is false evidence appearing real. She loves herself, she is grateful, stays connected to her higher self and to God. She knows her worth and acts like it. It takes practice but it's possible!

There are three key steps I took to become a dynamic woman. You can take them too!

First: I decided clearly what I wanted and what I didn't want. I decided to heal my past traumas, tell a new story, and see things differently. I told myself, "I want to live an extraordinary life. I want to own my power and take control of my mind. I want to live a life of travel; eating exquisite food, making unforgettable memories with my loved ones, and sharing my purpose to the world while getting very well paid for it."

Second: I understand who I truly am: a spiritual being having a human experience. God is the Creator, and we are made in the image of God—one with God with the same expansive, creative power. We can fully trust that we are unconditionally loved and supported. We will never be forsaken. Also, understanding the universal laws that hold this 3D universe together. Some of the most powerful ones are the laws of vibration, attraction, divine oneness, compensation, polarity, correspondence, inspired action, cause and effect, relativity, gender, perpetual transmutation of energy, and the law of rhythm. For every action, there is an equal and opposite reaction.

"Anything the mind of man can conceive, and bring itself to believe, it can achieve," says Napoleon Hill. Let yourself be guided by the all-knowing Spirit within you. Inspired action is taking the intuitive nudges you are given. Quiet your mind so you can understand when an inspired idea is coming and then act on that inspiration; that is the best action you can take! You are never alone: all the wisdom you need is inside of you.

Third: I surround myself with people who are where I want to be, who have the same values and want to better themselves as well. According to Karl Menninger, "Environment is more important than heredity." We naturally conform to our surroundings, so when you surround yourself with those who are operating at a level you want to be, you will start to pick up their habits, values, and mannerisms. This has been a game changer for me! Take audit of those who you are spending time with and think of who you can add to your circle of influence.

Starting with the first key to success is to clearly define your dream and decide that you will make it happen. Do this now! "What do you want your life to look like, or feel like? What do you want to do with your time, and who do you want around you?" The law of attraction is real. We attract with our thoughts and feelings—aka vibration. The thoughts we think, the feelings we have and the actions we take impact what is attracted to us, and how we act in the world.

This knowledge is powerful! We become what we think about. Thoughts are things. You can measure them; they give off a vibrational frequency, and each thought and each thing has its own frequency. We need to become an energetic match to the frequency of our desires. Einstein says, "Everything is energy; that is all there is to it. Match the frequency of the reality you want, and you cannot help but get that reality."

There are only two thought systems: fear and love. Choose love: choose to love yourself, love God, love your neighbor, love those that hurt you in the past, and do all you do with and for love. As we see the world, the world will be reflected back to us.

My hope for you is that you embrace the light that is within you; to be present in each moment, forgive all the mistakes you perceive you or someone else made from the past, and live at peace with who you are and where you are right now. Follow the above three steps to embrace the dynamic woman within you, and let her shine bright without borders or limits. You got this! Believe in yourself! Believe in **YOU!**

**Terri Wade** is a professional speaker, the founder of the Lady Entrepreneur Society, the host of Tuesdays with Terri, and author of the forthcoming book A-Z Happy. Terri is a former business professor. She has an MBA and is certified in Spiritual Life Coaching and 21st Century Leadership Skills.

Since 2010, Terri has helped thousands of entrepreneurs and businesses strategically grow their leadership ability, and create their ideal vision in order to grow themselves, their teams, and their company.

After working with Terri, her clients have transformed their mindset to courageously reach new heights in their sales. They have instilled success habits to exceed company goals, and become better team players to make the workday more enjoyable.

Learn more about Terri:

Email:Terri@terriwade.com

Instagram: Ladyentrepreneursociety

Website: https://www.terriwade.com/

Chapter 2

Resilience and Faith Personified
By Brenda Geary

There are many characteristics that define a dynamic woman as you will read and discover in this anthology. One specific characteristic that kept coming to the forefront of my mind as I thought about my life journey, is that a dynamic woman is resilient. A dynamic woman may fall down several times and pick herself back up every time because she knows that she has a purpose. Despite obstacles, her vision and faith propel her forward. As you read my story I invite you to think about the areas in your life where you can identify, and CELEBRATE your resilience.

I was born in Puerto Rico in the early 1960s. My Puerto Rican mother was two months pregnant with me when she met the airman that she would marry. He adopted me and my older sister and was the only father I knew.

They went on to have three additional children. I don't know anything about my biological father, not even his name. I often asked my mom about him but for whatever reasons she would not speak about him. My stepfather was stationed in Puerto Rico until I was six years old, and then we moved to the United States.

Sadly, I don't have a lot of memories from my childhood. Due to the repeated physical and verbal abuse I experienced from both parents, I have blocked out a lot of my childhood. My mother's cancer diagnosis and the subsequent surgeries took a huge physical and emotional negative toll on my mom & dad's relationship as well; and it seems like our family fell apart from that time forward. My father became an alcoholic and my parents fought continuously.

In order to escape the physical abuse, I learned to shrink and become invisible. I became the good girl, the people pleaser. It has taken me years of doing personal development work to release childhood programming. My coping mechanism for escaping the environment at home was to spend time with friends whose families' lives were stable and appeared to be nurturing. Additionally, a cornerstone of my life journey was when a neighbor invited me to her church.

When I walked into her church I found my home and I accepted the Lord as my Savior when I was 10 years old. From then on my faith has always been a guiding light in how I show up in the world. The Bible verse that I have always carried with me, and believe has been a part of my resilience story is, Hebrews 11:1— "Now Faith is the substance of things hoped for, the evidence of things not seen."

When I think about resilience I think of the young girl who actively sought out the safe environments and friends outside of her home that brought her a sense of peace. My mom was my first example of a dynamic woman. She was the embodiment of resilience. My mother, Carmen Maria Perez Rodriguez, will forever be my hero. I can proudly say that I am me, because of her. She was one of five children born in Puerto Rico to an abusive father, and a mother who never learned how to read or write. Their mother abandoned them as young children with their abusive father to save herself. My mother had to quit school in ninth grade in order to help her family with their finances.

An unexpected miscarriage in the mid-1970s revealed that she had pervasive ovarian cancer that led to a radical and trailblazing surgery. I remember taking her to the emergency room many times in the 15-20 years following her surgery, and the doctors were always in awe to see that she was alive when they saw the type of surgery that she had.

When my parents divorced in 1979, my father paid child support but it was not enough to support the four of us that were still at home. Despite the chronic pain following her cancer treatments, my mom figured out how to bring extra money into our home. She made her own clothes, worked at McDonald's, and worked as a housekeeper at the university. I am forever grateful to her for being an amazing role model, and for being my first example of a resilient dynamic woman. My mother taught me to never be afraid to learn the skills needed in order to make something work out.

My parents never talked about me going to college. We never had conversations about what was next or talked about careers. Thankfully, I was motivated to go to college because of the examples I saw from my closest circle of friends. It is absolutely true—your circle of friends has the ability to influence the direction of your life or the choices you make. A dynamic woman surrounds herself with those who have a plan and are going where she wants to go.

I was the only child in my family that went to college, and I earned both a Bachelor's in Communication and Master's in Human Resources. It brings me to tears when I think back to how proud my mother was of me when she attended both commencement ceremonies. I remember her saying, "Brenda, I'm not sure what all of this means but I think it must be a pretty big deal because of all those people standing on that stage with those fancy gowns on, and I am proud of you."

In my sophomore year of undergrad, I married and had a son the following year. My first husband and I divorced after a couple of years. My ex-husband was not a part of my son's life nor did he provide child support. When I think about resilience I think about being a single mom, attending college full time while working full time. As I reflect, I am grateful for the tough times that shaped me and I am so proud of the young man I raised.

After receiving my Master's in Human Resources, I went to work at a Fortune 500 company in their Executive Leadership Program. It was a program that only 1-2% of graduates went into. With knees knocking, being filled with self-doubts, a host of insecurities, and suffering from imposter syndrome, I stepped into Corporate America. I was fortunate to be assigned to an organization that had the only African American CEO and the only African American Senior Human Resources leader. These two leaders were amazing mentors. They helped me to understand the unwritten expectations of being a minority and a female within the corporate structure. Under their mentorship, I became a top performer in all of my positions and steadily received promotion after promotion. My corporate roles allowed me to travel to over 20 countries. This small-town girl from East Central Illinois has been able to see parts of the world that I never imagined.

In 2002 at the height of my career I had been promoted as the first-ever African American female in my division to achieve the Executive status. I loved my job and was excited about the future; and then life happened...BAM! Overnight my life changed and it would never be the same again. Life happened for me...read that again. It happened FOR ME not to me.

In June of 2004 I woke up one day with hives, welts, and rashes all over my body. There was non-stop itching. I literally never stopped itching from 2004 to 2011. My immune system crashed even further. I developed autoimmune issues: fibromyalgia, chronic fatigue syndrome, chronic vertigo and nausea. My body hurt so badly; I felt like my skin was on fire. At home I even wore my clothing inside out because seams hurt my body. I also developed cognitive dysfunction and lost my short-term memory. All of a sudden, I started to forget everything that I would say. I felt stupid and ashamed. Why could other executives operate at the highest levels without getting sick? Why did I get sick?

As a result of my health challenges I was forced to take a medical retirement because I could not function in my high level corporate role. At the time, I carried so much shame because my health issues resulted in my lack of performance. At my sickest I was in bed 20 hours a day, and was on 24 prescription medications. During that time I felt like I had lost myself. I forgot what it felt like to be Brenda; to be pain free and to be able to think. I was just existing—not really living. As I lay in bed in August of 2011, I prayed for a solution to my health struggles. Even though I was lying in bed in pain, **I knew that I was not done**; **I knew that I still had purpose in my life.**

My health story changed when I started to work with a team of holistic health professionals that taught me about the body's ability to heal with herbs. What I learned changed my life and fired me up. I started to live again, then another health challenge invaded my life in November of 2011. When I was diagnosed with cancer, I prayed and believed that God just had a stronger testimony for me to share. Chemotherapy and radiation therapy took me to some really dark places. At times I felt like I was in a dark cave just holding on to the cliff edge by my fingertips. Thankfully, God brought me through that challenge.

My mentor and coach taught me that sometimes our greatest gift comes wrapped in sandpaper. I absolutely believe that had I not gotten sick and had to find my way back from chronic pain and cancer, I would not be the person who I am today; with a passion to serve in the natural healing and neuro-transformational coaching space. I believe that my gift as a dynamic woman is wrapped in the fact that I have walked through the fire and now serve from a place of relatability for women dealing with chronic invisible illnesses, and the mindset challenges associated with chronic illness.

Today, I am pain free, prescription free, and cancer free. I love teaching women how to become the CEO of their own health journey; both physically and mentally. I pray that as you read my story, you were able to relate in some ways and were also able to identify and celebrate your resilience as a dynamic woman.

 **Brenda Geary** is a former corporate executive turned entrepreneur, motivational speaker and coach. After two decades as a successful human resource Vice President in a Fortune 500 Company, her world was turned upside down when she developed a number of autoimmune diseases and was also subsequently diagnosed with breast cancer. As a result of overcoming her health challenges, Brenda is now passionate about sharing her story of recovery and educating and inspiring others on how to achieve and maintain optimal wellness. Brenda lives in San Diego, CA and is married to the love of her life, Randy, and she has one son Michael that is the light of her life.

Connect with Brenda at:

Email: brenda@brendageary.com

Instagram and TikTok at BrendaGeary8

Chapter 3

Greatness Is Your Birthright
By Dr. Sue Carter Collins

I was born in 1951; the eighth child in a family of 10 children. I grew up in the Deep South during the height of American apartheid when Negro and Colored were the terms of the day. My daddy went to prison for killing a man shortly after I was born, and left Mama with a house full of children to raise. To say that we were extremely poor, would be an understatement. However, Mama was innately intelligent and extremely resourceful, and somehow, she kept us all together. Mama made sure that we were never hungry or without clothes, and we always had a place to stay. She was like a big protective bear who kept guard over her children. She was a strict disciplinarian and did everything in her power to impart wisdom to us. Mama hovered over and around us around the clock, keeping us safe until we could take care of ourselves.

As I reflect on what it means to be a dynamic woman, I think of my mama who passed away in 1988 but left behind a powerful legacy, which was, her love of education. Mama's shoulders are the ones that I stand on today. I want to believe that, because she had only completed the third grade, mama had an insatiable desire for learning. Some of my favorite memories are of the times when I sat on the floor between her legs as she combed my hair and told stories about her childhood. Mama loved school, but she only got to go when the weather was really cold, or when it snowed.

On those days she walked for miles to get to the one-room schoolhouse where all the children were taught together. When the weather was good, mama didn't go to school at all. Instead, she picked cotton and harvested tobacco in the fields with the other Colored children. Whenever mama told these stories the endings were always the same: sometimes she worked so hard that her hands bled, and the next day she would get up and do it all over again. As mama neared the ending of a story, a look of wistfulness would pass briefly over her face as she wished aloud that she had the opportunity to finish school. We kids would just laugh and say, "Tell us more mama!" Try as we might, we couldn't imagine living in the olden days. At that point, she would always admonish us to go to school and get an education. "Education is the key," she said. "They've got it and you can get it. Once you have it, it can never be taken away." Mama's words ignited a fiery desire in my heart for education that burns brightly to this day.

As I look back over my life, I stand amazed at my accomplishments and the number of college degrees I have attained. Given my family history, I was not supposed to do any of the things that I have done. Against all odds, this little black girl who grew up in the South, whose daddy was a convicted murderer, and whose mother was a field worker and an uneducated maid, finished high school. That little black girl even went beyond and attended college, completed five degrees, including a JD and a PhD. In each instance, I, that little black girl, was one of the first African Americans to integrate and graduate from these institutions.

Between 1973 and 2000, I held various positions in criminal justice including correctional officer, deputy sheriff, felony investigator, and law enforcement trainer. After completing law school in 1983, I was admitted to the Florida Bar Association and served as an appellate assistant public defender, assistant prosecutor, and independent legal consultant. In 1986, I became the first Police Legal Advisor for the Tallahassee, Florida Police Department—one of the largest agencies in the South. Given my daddy's criminal history, this was astounding!

I returned to college in 1994 and completed a PhD in Criminology and Criminal Justice in 2000. In 2001, I relocated to Atlanta where I accepted a tenure-track position as an assistant professor at Georgia State University Department of Criminal Justice and taught a variety of legal subjects. I earned tenure in 2008 and retired in 2015 as the first African American to be awarded emeritus associate professor status.

In total, I spent more than 40 years in law and criminal justice, in careers that kept me on the cutting edge of social change in a White male-dominated profession. While I am proud of the contributions I made in race and gender relations, I would be remiss if I did not say that it came at a great psychological cost. Often, mine was the only Black face in a sea of whiteness. The non-supportive nature of those in these environments took a toll on my self-esteem and my self-confidence. Despite my accomplishments, each day I felt like an imposter. I shrank to fit other people's perception that I wasn't good enough, or smart enough for the positions that I held. Over time, I began to believe the stories myself.

It is my belief that the body knows, and the body keeps score of all internal stressors that we do not acknowledge and address. In my case, after so many years of thinking I was okay, in 2004, I was stricken with Bell's Palsy, which is a stress-induced condition resulting in paralysis on the right side of my face. Although the condition has been partially cleared, I live with nerve damage for which there is no cure. In 2010, I suffered from respiratory issues that brought me near death. I was wheelchair-bound and unable to walk, and doctors have yet to identify the cause. I believe that it was stress related.

In 2012, after years of using alcohol to cope with stress and depression, I admitted to myself that I was an alcoholic. I could no longer stop drinking when I wanted to. As painful as it was, this acknowledgment pulled me back from the brink of suicide and started me on the path to healing. Today, I credit Alcoholics Anonymous for saving my life and reacquainting me with my true self and the dynamic woman that I am. AA is a spiritual program. In it, I met the God of my understanding and realized—perhaps for the first time—that I didn't have to do life alone.

While working on the 12 Steps of the AA program, I had to have some deep conversations with myself about myself, and where I came from. I had to reframe my story about my gender and the color of my skin. I had to reprogram my thinking and conversations about my self-worth, my intellectual abilities, my education, and my professional achievements for healing to take place. After struggling with these issues for so long, I had to learn to forgive myself, love myself, and trust myself for the unique and dynamic woman that I am.

As I continued to do the healing work of AA, I developed a deeper appreciation for life and my divine nature. Spiritual gifts that were long hidden began to emerge. I learned that I am highly intuitive and that I can hear and sense things that most people are not aware of. This realization fueled my desire to know more about spiritual metaphysics and, once again, I returned to school. In 2014 I completed a nine-month certification program and became a LifeWorks Certified Coach. Simultaneously, I was drawn to energy medicine and became a certified Reiki Master Teacher, Advanced Pranic Healer, Crystal Healing Practitioner, and Akashic Records Reader. In 2017, I completed a degree in metaphysics and became an ordained metaphysical minister.

Today I use all my skills and spiritual gifts to coach high-performing professional women to connect with their true selves, master their mindset, and release limiting beliefs that have hindered them from attaining their next-level goals. I coach around spiritual insights and strive to make the invisible visible. As a result of working with me, women have become empowered to break through mental barriers that have held them back and have successfully pursued their goals.

When I think of a dynamic woman, I think of a woman like me; one who has risen from humble beginnings. While each woman must arrive at her own definition, these are my thoughts.

- Shorn of titles, degrees, accolades, and masks, the dynamic woman is secure in her relationship with God. She knows the power of prayer. She is perfect in her imperfection and loves herself just as she is even as she strives to become a better person. She is not afraid to be her authentic self even when doing so is not pretty or popular.

- The dynamic woman feels connected to humanity. She moves through life sharing love and doing good wherever she goes. She strives to embody peace. She is committed to being light in a world that is filled with darkness.

- The dynamic woman is spiritually resilient. She is no stranger to life's ups and downs, or to its toils, troubles, and traumas. She has been broken in more ways than she can count and put back together in more places than she can remember. Though she is sometimes beaten down to the ground, the dynamic woman learns from each experience and never gives up. She derives strength from her faith and knows that God will never leave her or forsake her regardless of what life brings.

- Though the winds of fear and trepidation may blow, and the clouds of confusion and uncertainty may reign, the dynamic woman steps boldly into her greatness and plays fully out. She is clear on her purpose and knows her goals. She is in life for the long haul.

I AM a dynamic woman. I stand on my mother's shoulders. **Greatness is my birthright**. Today I embrace it. I encourage you to do the same.

Dr. Sue Carter Collins is a motivational speaker, spiritual teacher, energy healer, and a greatness life coach. She is originally from Gainesville, Florida and now resides in Atlanta, Georgia. She is the author of **Return to Self: 5 Keys to Emotional & Spiritual Freedom**, and owner of the Synergistic Healing Center of Atlanta. Dr. Collins speaks and trains on diverse leadership issues. She also coaches high-achieving women to connect with their authentic selves, release limiting beliefs, master their mindsets, and own their greatness so they can experience increased confidence, happiness, and success. Dr. Collins received a JD and PhD from Florida State University. She is an emeritus associate professor with Georgia State University and a retiree of the Florida Bar Association. She has authored numerous criminal justice articles and produces the PIVOT2GREATNESS Podcast.

Visit her website: www.syergistichealingcenter.com.

Call her: (770) 866-2608.

Email her: drsuecartercollins@gmail.com.

Follow her: FB, IG, and LI: @drsuecartercollins.

Chapter 4

When it Rains, Look for Rainbows
By Garri Davis

I would define a *Dynamic Woman* as a woman who motivates, who inspires, and who is a visionary. A *Dynamic Woman* is someone who leads with passion and integrity. She is simultaneously courageous and humble. A *Dynamic Woman* is disciplined, bold and emotionally intelligent. When I think of *Dynamic Women*, I think of Tamika Mallory, Michelle Obama, Angela Davis, Sojourner Truth, and my favorite entertainer, Beyonce. I also think of myself as a dynamic woman.

My name is Garri Davis and some of you may know that I own two successful child care businesses in Cincinnati, Ohio. I'm also a business coach. Through my training and development programs, I empower female entrepreneurs to identify and implement viable solutions to overcome risks in their organizations, so as to gain a greater understanding of how their businesses work and maximize profits.

As *Dynamic Women*, we sometimes make it look effortless. We make it look easy. No one understands the effort we put into our businesses behind the scenes. Even though people now consider my business a success, it has not always been this way. When I think about the road to success, I think about how difficult it was to find the financing that I needed to start my business and the lack of positive role models and mentors. There was a vast learning curve that I had to master in order to learn my business and how to generate profits.

During the spring of 2013, when I opened my first childcare center, for about a year, I was tired, stressed, and almost broken. My staff was underpaid and unmotivated; my enrollment was very low, and I could not afford the marketing required to increase enrollment in order to pay my staff, and myself, appropriately. As I sat in my office on a rainy day, with bills piling up, I heard water dripping inside the building. At first, it was a very slow drip.... drop..... drip....... drop, and then it became louder and heavier. I ran into a classroom and saw water pouring from the ceiling, and it smelled like old garbage. It was actually raining inside of the building. It had happened to be naptime, and the children were sleeping. I sprang into action while my mind drowned out the noise of the rain and teachers screaming. I transported the children from that classroom to another area of the building. That night I cried. I cried as hard as it had been raining inside of that building. I wanted to walk away; I wanted to give up and quit but I didn't. I worked long and hard to stop my business from, literally, sinking. The first thing I did was meet with the owners of the building, who blamed me, and took little to no responsibility for what had happened. I was told that I needed to figure it out, or get out!

I knew then that I would have to lean in on my leadership skills: I have always been in leadership roles, even when I worked in the corporate sector. In the corporate world and as an entrepreneur, I have found myself in situations where I have been surrounded by people who don't look like me: they had no qualms letting me know that I didn't measure up to their standards; making me feel small and insignificant. We tend to allow others to place limitations on what we can achieve. Being a leader in my own organization, I have faced similar challenges.

Has there ever been a time when you have been told, "No, this won't work," or "You don't know what you are doing"? Maybe you just felt like quitting. Has there ever been a time when, despite your best efforts, people see you as less than, undeserving, and not worthy? Well, I have experienced that too, and on more than one occasion. The key is not to give up; to not lie down just to be walked over. The key is to find the *Dynamic Woman* in you. **The key is to get up! Stand up! and speak up**!

This experience marked the beginning of my journey to becoming a *Dynamic Woman*. There were so many things that I had to learn, and although the learning curve was very steep, I knew that for me to succeed, I would need to figure out a way to overcome these obstacles. One of the first things I did was to invest in professional development, which introduced me to various systems that I could implement in order to save time, and eventually save money. This helped me in becoming a more efficient and influential businesswoman. From studying other successful business owners, I knew that I would need to understand my business inside and out. After many hours of professional development, I finally felt adequately informed and astute about where my business matters were concerned.

The second part of my journey towards becoming a *Dynamic Woman* was something that I just stumbled upon. In August of 2019, I was supposed to be at a childcare conference, but instead, I went to a conference on speaking and writing and learned about personal development. From this conference, I signed up for a retreat. During the retreat, I focused on myself; something I had never done in my entire life. I learned my strengths, my weaknesses, and my triggers. I laughed and cried a lot! It was the best investment that I had ever made in myself.

I walked away with a strength that I never knew I had. I was more confident, and I had a heightened awareness of who I was. I learned to shine from the inside out. To some people, I was unrecognizable. I was transformed into a *Dynamic Woman*!

With professional and personal development under my belt, I knew I could face my challenges equipped with the necessary tools to overcome just about anything in my path.

I think back to 2012 when I decided that if I was going to work hard, be stressed out, and have sleepless nights, I might as well open my own business. That's just what I did. All of the work was not in vain.

I have had poor employees, so I created a system to hire better employees.

I had low enrollment, so I found more efficient ways to market and grow my business. I couldn't pay myself, so I found a way to partner with other organizations to help my business grow and increase my cash flow significantly.

Believe in yourself. Your hard work and dedication will pay off!

As far as being a *Dynamic Woman* goes, there are going to be peaks and valleys. Of course, that is my life story. I accept each challenge head-on and always remain professional and upbeat. I try to listen more than I speak and, most of all, I maintain confidence in my ability to lead.

So, now I can stand before you as a *Dynamic Woman* with two successful childcare businesses and a lucrative training and coaching business. I am also a transformational speaker, and an Amazon best-selling author. If I can do all of this, you certainly can too.

There is no secret sauce, but there are three things that you can do to uncover the Dynamic Woman in you.

1. Be resilient—Things are going to happen. Don't take things personally; stay focused on your goals.
2. Be grateful—Appreciate the small things.
3. Never give up—Will it get hard? Yes, but will it be worth it? Absolutely!

Garri Davis is a native of Cincinnati, Ohio with a Master's Degree from Wesleyan University where she graduated Cum Laude.

She is the Owner & CEO of Water Lily Learning Centers and the CEO of The Garri Davis Agency where she is a transformational strategic business coach: supporting driven and ambitious female entrepreneurs who are ready to step out and increase their possibilities to design the life of their dreams.

Garri is a transformational speaker & the author of the amazon best-selling book CEO in Stilettos.

She is also a partner in LeadH.E.R. Events which provides business leadership conferences for women, and Brown Girls Real Estate Group.

Contact Garri today to explore how to make positive impacts on your business!

Email.: www.garridavisagency.com

Website: www.garridavis.com

LinkedIn: https://www.linkedin.com/in/garridavis/

Chapter 5

*The Journey to Discovering (J.O.Y)
Just Own You - From Fear to
Abundance*

By Joy LaBelle

A s I sit and begin writing about the Dynamic Woman that I am, I pause to send messages to my dear family and friends; letting them know that I love them and how grateful I am to have them in my life. I want to ensure that they know and feel how special they are to me, and how just thinking of them warms my heart. I now reflect on the amount of personal development and healing work I've done over the years on myself—to now having amazing human loves in my life.

Wow! As I reflect on who I am now, I smile, and a warm sensation fills my entire being. I'm living my purpose and showing up in every aspect of my life as me. Who is "me"?

I am Joy LaBelle, an amazing mother, Fortune 500 Senior Corporate Leader, International Personal Development Coach, International Certified Mindfulness Facilitator/ Teacher, and someone who lives and breathes in the joys of life daily as a Dynamic Woman.

I must not forget to mention that I, Joy, am also a world traveler, a skydiver, a lover of water, air, and earth, and I can go on and on because I am genuinely limitless and living my life unapologetically, discovering a more profound love for Joy daily, and helping others to discover their J.O.Y (Just Own You). Just Own You is the process of *Just Breathe/Be, Own your whole self, and You will experience life more abundantly.*

It sounds unattainable, huh? to be able to wake up loving the skin you are in and the life you have created daily. I would never have imagined that this life was possible. You see, my journey, as I think back, began around 2012 when I started asking God, the Universe, "What is your will for my life? I literally would cry at the thought of me. Yes, I was well accomplished; however, I was walking around feeling like I was carrying the weight of the world on my shoulders. To top it off, I walked around with a knot in my throat, full of fear and anxiety— the type of anxiety that builds when you begin to speak: the words that escape are pure nothingness or sound like Linus from Charlie Brown "Wonk Wonk Wonk Wonk." The anxiety would build in my throat, even more, the huge pressure in my head would build, and the lump in my throat would pulsate stronger and stronger. Where did my voice go? Where did my logic go? *where? where? where*? raced through my mind, and still no words escaped.

Even with my accomplishments, I still woke up most mornings, rolled out of bed, walked to the bathroom, looked in the mirror, and was disgusted at the person staring back at me. Then, the tears would begin to fall. I cried because I still heard the names I was called by loved ones and classmates. The song would peer into my mind, "Joy to the World Oink Oink the Lord has Come." I could also hear my parents calling me fat, or, here's a good one: "You look smart until you open your mouth." All of these memories still showed up at the most inopportune times.

I recall a time when I started a new position in leadership around 2010 as a Senior Manager; I was nervous and excited as I walked into a meeting with my peers and other executives. I proceeded to say hello to those in the room, and I was ignored and told that I could not sit at the table because guests sat on the outer perimeter. The voices from my childhood were pestering my mind, and now this new confirmation that I didn't fit in or belong. You see, I am a black woman that has always worked in white male dominant industries, so I had become accustomed to not fitting in, and over time that began to silence me more and more.

In 2014, my anxiety had gotten worse, and I was beginning to experience severe migraines and blurred vision. At this point, I was feeling depressed and felt like a failure in all areas of my life. See, at the time, I was a military wife in a rocky marriage, and my now ex-husband had been on several tours abroad. When he was away, our relationship was great; however, when he came home, the relationship would always become strained for my oldest son and me, for sure—the youngest was too young to notice the shift.

I remember in November of 2014, the family and I took a trip to Maui, Hawaii. It was a fantastic trip where we snorkeled, snuba-dived, 15 feet deep, with a tank on top of the water. We explored the island, and then we returned home. Shortly after my return, I had a pre-scheduled spa appointment to receive my monthly massage. It was a love that I had discovered over the years that helped me to destress. As I lay on the table, my mind would not quiet, I heard my internal voice taking over. *Why am I living this life? Why am I not supported? why...? why...?why...? Shut up, I'm trying to relax and destress!* The voices continued until my time was up. As I drove home I passed a sign that read, Psychic Readings, which was in bold lights. I immediately remembered hearing that Psychics are fake, and an evil work of the devil in my mind.

As I drove by, I captured the number and immediately ignored the voices because I needed answers. I was still upset because I was not able to fully enjoy my massage due to the heated discussion that occurred at home right before I left. I was tired of this feeling, and I yearned to understand why. I called the number while still driving and was able to make an appointment the same day. This was unknowingly the beginning of how I learned how to "Just Breathe".

How do you Just Breathe? was my first thought, or even, how do you Just Be? Breathing happens automatically. I hadn't thought to notice it, or even if I was doing it correctly; because in my head we are born, and after the spank on the behind from the doctor, we begin to breathe automatically. That is what I knew at the time, however, I was being led to learn how to spend time with myself and learn how to discover my answers from within. Still searching, I went to a second spiritual advisor that led me to a Medi-Healer who had this 21-day Medi-healing virtual program that would help me begin to heal from generational trauma. I had never meditated before; however, I began meditating in January 2015 and meditated twice a day with this spiritual meditation healer, and I began to discover how to love myself more and more each day with each session. I would even travel to see this fantastic healer in person. I was committed to finding answers.

In 2015 I found my freedom from living in darkness and self-hate for most of my life, looking outside of me for God and not realizing how to connect with Him fully. I then learned how to spend quiet time with Him through meditation. Meditation supported me through my divorce, which began in 2015, and helped me connect with my sons differently. I stopped trying to control everything outside of me and began to love myself. I started over with my two sons. I still walked around with the knot in my throat, so I continued to meditate, and my world opened me up to more spiritual healers and more awakenings. I even released about 70 lbs of excess weight and stress. I am still on my journey and I have now realized how Just Breathing or Just Being has changed how I see myself, and I am now diving deeper into discovering Joy.

At the end of 2016, I unknowingly began to seek an understanding of how to "**O**wn my whole self". I joined a program where I had to develop my life purpose statement. I sat for days in the dark of the night praying to God and meditating. Finally, as I was writing, I felt the hairs on my skin rise, and I began to write my purpose. My purpose was to help heal and awaken the world to God's love and power. I had no idea of how I would accomplish this; however, it brought a smile to my face, and warmth resonated throughout my body. At the end of the program, a peer in the class recommended reading a book by Lisa Nichols titled, Abundance Now. This was my first time hearing about this author. As I read through the book, I connected with this author very strongly because we had similar weight loss journeys. I loved the book, and I began following the author. I had the honor of meeting her in person for the first time in January 2017 at Agape Christian Center.

"Shortly after the retreat, I experienced other life challenges. However, I had begun the healing that helped me handle many life challenges. I committed in 2017 to serve in as many events and conferences as I could, sharing my healing story. I now had a community of genuine people who loved me and saw me in a different light; I knew I was enough and truly began experiencing life more abundantly. In 2018, I became a certified Pranic Healer. In 2019, I started my journey of deep-diving into meditation and became an Internationally Certified Mindfulness Teacher in February 2021. As a Mindfulness Personal Development Coach, I am committed to helping others tap into a power greater than them through meditation, mindfulness, and healing. By learning to Just Breathe, Own your whole self, You will experience life more abundantly. This, alone with my just being me makes me a Dynamic Woman who grew through my pain into my greatness.

Joy LaBelle is a Mindfulness Personal Development coach and founder of Joy Unleash Ur Potential, LLC. She's a Trained Mindfulness Facilitator through UCLA Mindful Awareness Research Center (MARC). She's a Certified Mindfulness Teacher, Professional (CMT-P) by the International Mindfulness Teachers Association. Through her coaching and mindfulness sessions, she creates compassionate, loving spaces for individuals to self-heal from the inside out. Joy holds a B.S. in Electronics Engineering, two Master's Degrees, and certifications in Pranic Healing and Trauma-Sensitive Mindfulness. Joy has over 20 years of experience leading and growing organizations.

Joy lives in Huntington Beach with her two amazing sons. Joy is committed to helping others tap into a power greater than themselves through meditation, mindfulness, and healing. By learning to *Just* be, *Own* your whole self, *You* will experience life more abundantly.

To contact Joy LaBelle, please see below:
Email: joyunleashurpotential@gmail.com
Website: www.joyunleashurpotential.com
IG: unleash_ur_potential
Facebook: Joy UnleashUr Potential
LinkedIn:https://www.linkedin.com/mwlite/in/adamsjoyl

Chapter 6

The Dynamic Woman
By Ene Obi

d_{ynamic}
/dʌɪˈnamɪk/

By Ene Obi

Dynamic (of a person): positive in attitude and full of energy and new ideas (Source: Google)

Words like 'change', 'progress', and 'activity' are often associated with the word 'dynamic'.

What makes a dynamic woman?

A dynamic woman recognises that life in the 21st century is challenging, especially since the year 2020. Life before 2020 was eminently different. For the dynamic woman, life in 2022 and beyond, will be very different. She will be the best version of herself and get uncomfortable with the current version. A dynamic woman has questions right now for which she doesn't have all the answers because the answers she has are based on her current life. She knows that she cannot simply copy and paste these answers because if she did, she'd be stuck in her past.

A dynamic woman gives herself permission to get uncomfortable sometimes. She knows she cannot become a game changer, impacting anyone's life, not even her own, if she doesn't explore and step outside her comfort zone to do something she's never done before.

The year 2020 presented many women with choices. A lot of people were suffering. Aside from the obvious devastation of human loss, there was further distress caused by job loss, potential job loss, eviction, insecurity, fear, anxiety, depression, and uncertainty.

Sometimes we encounter difficult situations which we think are so huge; situations that have the potential to break us, and we cannot see the way out of. We haven't got the skills or experiences to deal with challenges of this scale, and so we feel powerless because we don't see a way out. It is often in these situations that lie the 'hidden' opportunity for us to metamorphose into becoming dynamic.

How do I know this? I know because this is a place where I once lived. In 2001, I left a great corporate job in one of the world's most prestigious investment banks to set up a business. Three years later, that business failed, leaving me and my family with over GBP100k in debt. I had more debt than I could think of making. I was buried in debt.

The failure of that business dealt me a heavy blow. For a long time, life looked bleak. I would lie in bed with the curtains closed, blackening out the room; crying out; begging for help. At one point, I'm ashamed to say that I even contemplated taking my own life. To me, that was the easiest way out of the mess that I'd created for my family and myself.

The business failure stripped me of all self-respect. I was riddled with a deep sense of guilt, shame, loss, humiliation, and ineptitude. I was responsible for bringing this situation to my family. I had failed financially, personally, and professionally—I was a failure. "My family would be better off without me, the failure," I told myself.

With the love and support of my mother, husband, and siblings, I started to slowly draw strength and faith from them, as well as from life itself. There were many days when this was almost impossible, but the smiles on the faces of my sons were enough to make me believe there was hope. I lived for those smiles. I clung on to life because of their smiles and hugs. They were too young to understand what was going on and I didn't want them to sense that there was a problem. That only added to my shame and made me feel like a failure—I'd let them down. I believe that your children being disappointed in you as a result of your actions has got to be one of the most humiliating experiences a parent could have.

I eventually got a job and slowly, knuckled down to work. We then started chipping away at our debt, focusing on what needed to get done and set about getting it done.

By the year 2010, approximately 5 years after the business failed, we were completely debt-free. The secured mortgage was paid off along with every financial obligation we had: credit cards, store cards—everything. We remain debt-free up to today. Now, the same banks which wouldn't bail us out: those who were constantly chasing us with repayment reminders are still chasing us—except now they're chasing us to extend us credit! No thank you 'Mr. Bank', I'm doing well all by myself! It's interesting how banks want to lend money to people who don't need their money!

As I write this chapter, it is January 2022 and we have regained everything we lost—many times over. Now, I share this experience, about the tears I shed and the lessons I learned, not as a burden but as a tool to be used as a blueprint, a survival guide, to help other people who are going through similar circumstances. I realise that true strength is found when you are able to regain strength and rise again, after being knocked down. You might be temporarily incapacitated but not permanently defeated! **That is a dynamic woman.**

Here are the lessons I learned about being a dynamic woman.

1. There are times when you may need to borrow someone else's belief in you until your belief in yourself kicks in. When you are down, remember that you are not broken; you are not out. Accept the situation and take responsibility for where you are and for your next move. It is your life, and you have to direct it and not let external factors move you out of alignment with who you are and where you want to go.

2. Never try to solve a temporary situation with a permanent solution. Do not take drastic actions on anything. Trust the process and allow things to unfold in time. Whatever defeat, hopelessness, despair, or devastation you may be going through, will pass. There is a saying that goes, "When you're going through adversity, keep going." I am stronger than I thought I was. What doesn't break you makes you stronger. You are stronger than you think you are, and you will come through. You'll probably be amazed at just how strong you are.

3. Whatever you may be going through, think of your life as a book, with different chapters. Today is the end of the current chapter and tomorrow, you will start the next chapter. You can't start a new chapter of your life if you keep re-reading the last one. You've read it enough times, it's time

to move on. The difference is that, with this new chapter, you are in control. You are the author of your story. You are the hero of your life. You need to write the story the way YOU want it to go. So, hold your head up high, take a beautiful-looking pen and start writing the next chapter of your life.

4.   Give yourself permission to move with consistency and at a momentum that's sustainable to you. You're not building your next year; you're building your lifetime legacy. Take your time. Be on fire about your implementation. Ask yourself what you can apply today to show that you learned yesterday. Give yourself permission to make small but consistent moves.

5.   Gratitude will help to focus the mind. At all times and in all things, we should remember the blessings that are in our lives and show gratitude.

6.   You have to believe that things are going to get better, in spite of what you're going through. Refocus your mind. Think of the things you've overcome; the things you have been through and the victories gained. Take your strength from these memories and let them give you hope, knowing if you could get through those things, you can get through whatever you're going through now. Look back on your life and see what

you've overcome and how far you've come. This will give you courage with what you're dealing with right now.

7. Don't compare yourself with anyone. Don't compare your beginning with someone else's middle or end, and then say you're not doing it right. Don't think that the filtered story of someone else's life that you see online is the whole story—Don't look to the left or right. **Keep your eyes on your life and the goal you have set for your life.** That's where your prize is.

'I don't like to gamble. But if there is one thing I am willing to bet on, it's myself.'

~Beyonce

A dynamic woman is prepared to bet on herself. **Bet on you.**

Ene Obi is an International TEDx Speaker, best-selling author, coach, and consultant who specializes in working with personally and professionally successful women, who want to create a life with more meaning, impact, and significance.

For almost three decades Ene had a corporate career at global organizations including Visa, HBSC, AstraZeneca, and Goldman Sachs.

With a deep desire to do something more personally meaningful, she has set up Ziano Mindspa, where she uses her story, experience and expertise to help career professionals develop clarity, courage, commitment, and conviction to reimagine their lives, and birth new dreams as they create their Next Chapter.

Ene Obi has shared global stages with world-renowned speakers including: Les Brown, Dr. Cheryl Wood and Lisa Nichols.

Ene Obi can be contacted via:
Website: www.ziano.co.uk
Instagram: ziano_mindspa
Facebook: zianomindspa

Chapter 7

She Rises, Resilient, Responsible & Sovereign

By Tanya Sherise Odums

When I hear the word dynamic, for some reason I think of dynamite–a powerful, explosive force– a substance that destroys but creates the space to rebuild from a place of nothingness. So, when I reflect on what it means to be a dynamic woman, I think of the women in my life: my elders and ancestors that came before me. These women struggled and have been through some things that would have destroyed most; yet they have overcome... crafting the blueprint that inspired me to be a dynamic force: a vital resilient woman who continues to persevere and prevail over the trials, and tribulations of life.

So, who is a Dynamic Woman? She is a woman who takes full responsibility for her life. She does not make excuses or quit when the going gets tough. She is self-defined and rules her life, knowing that she has the power to create whatever she wants under any circumstance. She is willing to weather the storm no matter how hard it gets. No matter how many times life knocks her down, she is determined to get up and move through the darkness to get to the other side where her sunshine dwells. She is SOVEREIGN!

Sometimes it is hard for me to embrace that I am a dynamic woman due to the old toxic beliefs that stem from my complex trauma history. My trauma is rooted in grief, loss, abandonment, rejection, and betrayal. These stem from my experiences with domestic violence, molestation, and rape. In addition to the loss of my parents and two children through miscarriages—I have been through a lot. However, I have chosen to share the story of the rite of passage I went through as my mother made her transition from this earth. It was this experience that impacted my life the greatest to date and taught me how to be a resilient, responsible, and sovereign woman. My story of grief and loss began at the age of five after my parents separated and my father committed to a new relationship. My father took full responsibility for raising a ready-made family, yet neglected his responsibility to/for me. The greatest trauma of all, was the death of the love of my life: my mother, Zenobia Griffin Odums. Although this loss was over 30 years ago, the tears still stream as I craft my words to tell this story that shaped my life.

I was 15 years old when my mother was diagnosed with cervical cancer– she was only 35. During the two years I spent caring for her; I watched her deteriorate and that slowly chipped away at my spirit. I remember getting up in the middle of the night to give her medicine. I rubbed her back as she screamed in pain. I was unaware that my mother was dying, and I can remember her preparing me to be responsible and independent; showing me how to write checks to pay the rent and her life insurance each time she was hospitalized. On June 14, 1989, at the young age of 37, my mother took her last breath, relieving the family of the decision to put her on life support. I was only 17 years old and had just completed my first year of college. I was in denial. My mother never uttered a word about her terminal illness. Then it happened—she was taken away from me.

My entire life changed that dreadful day as my grandmother said, "Tanya your mother died." I was in shock, and disbelief. I walked to the kitchen and had a tantrum like a two-year-old; throwing myself on the floor and repeatedly screaming, "I want my mother back!" My cousin, Jackie, pulled me up from the floor and held me in his arms, as I sobbed uncontrollably. I had never felt such pain.

The real wailing began as I sat on the steps at the back door of my nana's house that night, while talking on the phone with my best friend, Tanya White. The tears would not stop. I struggled to embrace the reality that I would never see my mother again; never hear her voice, nor hug or kiss her ever again. That's when the grief came to a head. I literally felt my heart breaking slowly down the middle and I have never been the same emotionally or spiritually since. My world was shattered, and I had to figure out how to pick the pieces up and put them back together without my mommy.

Assuming full responsibility for myself and my life, I prepared my mother for her final rite of passage and laid her to rest. Little did I know, on that day, I too was being prepared for my greatest rite of passage into adulthood. I became a full-grown woman that day.

As I moved through this rite of passage, attempting to rebuild my life, and envision my future, no words could describe the depths of depression my soul experienced. I struggled with feelings of anger, rage, sadness, hopelessness, loneliness, and despair. Despite all of those dark, heavy feelings, it was at that moment that I realized that my life belongs solely to me, and it would become whatever I created it to be. Despite how I felt, I showed up for myself and did not become stagnant because of my pain. I kept on moving forward in faith; even when I had to crawl and sometimes felt crippled by my emotions. I sought out the life lessons on this journey each step of the way.

The three greatest lessons I learned from the death of my mother—embarking on this rite of passage into womanhood are:

1. **Resiliency:** Life is about choices. No matter how hard life gets I still have the power to choose how to move through the challenges. In order to be resilient, I must make good choices and be willing to weather the storm.

2. **Responsibility:** I am responsible for my life and must be willing to take full responsibility for it, no matter what curveball life throws at me. Despite how I feel, I must handle my business as feelings are not facts. Just because I am experiencing pain and anger, does not give me the right to destroy my life by making poor choices.

3. **Sovereignty:** I am the goddess of my life. I have supreme power and authority over my life. I have the ability to create my reality, and life is whatever I choose to make it! I have a choice: I can wallow in my misery and stay stuck or do the work to move through, and craft a grand vision for my future without my mother. This I would do, knowing that I am protected and divinely guided because I am tapped into an unlimited divine source, which I call the universe.

In short, this experience forced me to exercise my sovereign power by taking responsibility for my life. As a woman who comes from a lineage of resilient, authentic, fearless, confident, and self-reliant, yet interdependent women, I have come to understand that, in every challenge I face, there is a lesson to be learned. I also understand that I have the power to apply these lessons and use them to aid in my transformation into the successful Dynamic Woman I have evolved into today.

In the spirit of transparency, I want to share that I am currently in the midst of weathering yet another storm. I am emotionally triggered because I am currently reliving my childhood trauma as I care for my 92-year-old grandmother, whose health has suddenly declined. I am trying to manage all of the same dark feelings I had as a teenager witnessing my mother's decline. I feel defeated but the Dynamic Woman within will not give up. **I am choosing to stand, despite feeling like I want to fall**.

So, to all the dynamic men and women struggling right now, I encourage you to keep moving forward, despite what you feel. As you continue to embark on this journey, I want to share five takeaways you can embrace from my story of resilience and perseverance:

1. **Trauma does not define you** and does not have to ruin your life. It is an experience you can overcome if you put in the work and seek your lessons in the midst of the storm. Do not give up!

2. **You are responsible for your life** regardless of what is going on. Seek the help you need to get through the hard times.

3. **Raise your standards and expectations of yourself.** You are stronger than you think. Don't be afraid to stand on your own two feet; especially when you lack social support. Believe in your ability to get through the tough times.

4. **Always stand in your inner goddess** and strive to be the best version of yourself despite what you are going through.

5. **You are unlimited.** There are no limits except the ones you place on yourself— in your mind. Whatever you put your mind to you can achieve, but you have to be willing to put in the work and believe in your heart that it is achievable. There will be times when you will struggle and fail. That's life and part of the process of personal growth and expansion. It is possible to make a way out of no way. So, when life appears to be blowing up and your world seems to be crumbling around you, just know YOU have the power to rebuild from a place of nothingness by tapping into your inner goddess who is connected to the greater powers of the universe. Despite how you may feel, despite how many times you do not meet the mark, keep trying and remember YOU ARE UNLIMITED! **You are dynamic.**

Tanya Sherise Odums is a Licensed Clinical Social Worker and Certified Clinical Trauma Professional, specializing in the treatment of depression and trauma. She was born and raised in Brooklyn, New York and has over 25 years of experience working with NYC's most vulnerable populations in a variety of private and city institutions. She is the founder of *KhepeRa Counseling and Consulting Licensed Clinical Social Work Services* and *HYPE: Helping Young People Excel, Inc.* Tanya is a former professor of Psychology and Human Services at Touro College and the City University of New York; and former Adjunct Lecturer for New York University's Silver School of Social Work Advanced Trauma-Informed Clinical Practice Program.

Tanya is a Mental Health Mentor and Transformation Coach, who helps people turn their trauma into triumph through taking responsibility for their lives: teaching them how to master their minds, and manage depression, so they can craft the lives they want and deserve.

To contact Tanya, please see below.

Facebook @ TanyaSheriseOdums

Instagram: @khepeRa_Heals

Email: KhepeRaHeals@gmail.com

Websites: www.TanyaSheriseOdums.com

www.KhepeRaHeals.org

Chapter 8

My Journey to Self-Discovery
By Dr. Brandy Florence

A dynamic woman is one who walks to the beat of her own drum, knows what she wants, and isn't afraid to go after it. No, she may not achieve the goal the first, second, or even 10th time; but once she's made up her mind nothing will stop her. She learns to pivot when necessary. She doesn't lose sight of the goal, sure she'll get discouraged and told "NO" more times than "YES" but deep down she knows she is destined for so much more. She is humble, patient, and kind to those along the way because she understands they are all a part of the journey. She doesn't always see herself as a dynamic woman, so she must learn to see herself through the lenses of others at times. What she does comes naturally to her, and she may not recognize the gift that's on the inside of her, but it's there. Who is the dynamic woman? Surely not me?

My story doesn't look like this or that person's: my struggle wasn't tough, I've never been homeless living in a car, never had to pull myself out of the mud, or had a dysfunctional or traumatic childhood. Therefore, how could I compare myself with those who have gone through so much, and label myself a dynamic woman? That's the problem! We often compare our story to others and decide it's not good enough. Being a dynamic woman often comes at a cost; usually long periods of isolation to hear your thoughts and gain clarity. You will lose friends and family along the way, often misunderstood and made to feel bad about your decisions, because the shift will cause you to change.

Growing up I was always so focused on my goals that I feel like I missed out on truly living and enjoying the journey to womanhood. Life is a journey full of ups and downs, which we need to process as they come. I was conditioned to get over it and push through so much that I didn't take the time to adjust. I attribute this behavior to my early experience with the death of my grandmother. After her death, nothing could have been more traumatic to me than death; so "get over it and move on" became my mindset. I didn't allow myself the grace to really learn, fail or explore. Being the oldest I felt a responsibility to always be the "good one" and do things right, and when I did something wrong it wasn't discussed.

The truth of the matter is, it's: My Story—My Journey—My Truth. I didn't always see myself as a dynamic woman. When I first heard about this project, I was very hesitant to tell my story. Yes, I've made some great accomplishments in my life, but that does not qualify me as a Dynamic Woman.

Although today I am considered a dynamic woman to many, I began as a broken little girl. Being the oldest granddaughter, some would say I was the favorite: the one who went on trips with my grandparents and pretty much got what I asked for. Life was great. I was a normal kid who stayed out of trouble and did as I was told; until the day the perception of me changed; at least in my mind it did. One Saturday afternoon, when I was 12 years old, I was at a friend's house with the boys. They were like big brothers, so we often hung out; no big deal, right? Well, that Saturday was different. I was gone longer than expected so my father drove around the corner looking for me. When he pulled up my heart sank, and I knew immediately I was in trouble. Did I mention that I was sitting on one of the boys' laps when he pulled up? I couldn't explain this one away, so I jumped up quickly. My father didn't say a word. That ride around the corner felt like an eternity: nothing was said and when we pulled up, he just told me to go to my room.

That wasn't the worst of the story. Sure, my dad was disappointed, and my mother was upset. Just when I thought it had passed, I went to grandma's house not thinking anything out of the norm—I mean I was always at grandma's house. It wasn't until she told me to have a seat at the formal dining table that I realized that something wasn't right. It was dim in the house aside from the natural light from the big living room window. It was eerily quiet in the house since the house was usually full of people—my cousins, aunts, and uncles. I mean, grandpa wasn't even home. My grandma sat across the table from me and began to tell me that what I did was not ladylike and that little girls shouldn't sit on boys' laps. I was crushed and disappointed in myself. That's when the shift occurred in my mind, I didn't ever want to be the girl to disappoint the family; especially grandma—ever again. Well, I never had the chance to right my wrongs, because Grandma passed away about six months later. I was devastated. I remember falling to my knees at the funeral thinking, *now she'll never get a chance to see that I am not the little girl who goes around just sitting on boys' laps.* This was the beginning of the perfect granddaughter syndrome— there was no room to mess up.

From that point on, my life became accomplishment driven. I had to prove myself: I wouldn't be the first one to shack up with my boyfriend; get pregnant before marriage, or the one who didn't complete college. I honed in on my skill sets and learned the importance of hard work, dedication, perseverance and resilience. I set a goal in mind and didn't stop until I achieved it—the true definition of tenacity. It started at the age of 16 when I graduated high school—I did it in three years. I started college with the goal of becoming a cardiologist. That is when I first recall saying to myself, *I wish grandma was here to see me now.* I then realized that it was because Grandma was big on education. She would have been so proud of me. After obtaining the first degree, things didn't go as planned so I had to pivot, and went back to pursue my master's degree—becoming the first in the family to obtain a graduate degree. Once again, the little voice in my head said, *Man, I wish grandma was here to see me now.*

After graduating I started my career, then I went on to purchase my first home. I was really doing it, then the little voice came back in my head again. It wasn't until I was about 28 years old that I realized that all these years I have been emotionally stuck as the 12-year-old trying to right my wrongs. My "good girl" image was ruined with my grandma and when she left this earth, I've been trying to prove that I am so much more. I've had tunnel vision ever since I was that little girl. I've been so focused on the career grind, goals, and success that I neglected relationships, that I desired and barely watered them. What my experiences have taught me is that everything in life that we want to flourish needs to be cared for and watered just like flowers. Sure, I accomplished my goals but at what cost? The journey has been lonely. Had I allowed myself to enjoy the journey and give myself grace to grow, fail, pivot and love without fear it may have been more enjoyable.

So, my advice to anyone as they navigate this journey of life...

- Don't allow anyone's perception of you to hold you hostage, as I did for so many years. It doesn't matter how you start but how you finish. Stop comparing your story to others. Everything you need is already inside of you. Take time and learn to pivot to get to where you want to be.
- Get quiet: spend some time with yourself, and develop healthy habits. Don't get discouraged despite the beginnings, and don't hold back in fear of what anyone thinks or says about you.
- Trust the process, and walk away from those things that no longer serve you in this season of life. Take the time you need to process the shifts along the way. The world needs you—just as you are.

So, now when I ask myself, "Who is a dynamic woman?" I quickly reply, "ME!" I am a dynamic woman. You are a dynamic woman as well. You see, it's a mindset shift, not just a story.

Today, I am walking in my purpose: helping women to discover their authentic selves. As a result of working with me, women learn to live their lives "full out" unapologetically, letting go of the things that have been keeping them stagnant and stuck. Resiliency becomes their normalcy.

Dr. Brandy Florence has over 15 years in healthcare operations: working in various roles, ranging from consulting to performance improvement. She is now working in her current role as—hospital administrator. These roles have led her down many paths where she has experienced her own journey through the power of resiliency.

She was born and raised in Los Angeles, California, where she still currently resides. She obtained her doctorate from USC in the year 2020. Dr. Brandy Florence is also the published dissertation author of, "Missed Opportunities: Lack of Advancement of African American Females into Senior Executive Healthcare Leadership."

She is now a professional certified life coach who specializes in **resiliency**. She helps her own clients navigate through their journey of resiliency in the areas of relationships, life, career, and education. Through her program, you will learn how to make "**Resiliency Your Normalcy**".

Instagram: @theresiliency_coach

Email: theresiliencycoachbflo@gmail.com

Calendar for a free discovery session: https://drbflo. as.me/discoverycall

Chapter 9

The Spiritual Journey to Becoming Dynamic
By Jackie V. Harden

Dynamic: (of a person) positive in attitude and full of energy and new ideas.

Woman: woman, female, lady, are nouns for **an adult female human being**; one paradigm of gender and biological sex for adult female human beings. Woman is the general term.

Faith: "Now faith is the substance of things hoped for and the evidence of things not seen."- Hebrews 11:1

I'm not a scholar, doctor, scientist, preacher, or inventor; although I did graduate from the School of Hard Knocks. In that case, I guess you could say I got my PhD in Life's Experiences. To date, being a mom and breaking the cycle of child abuse are my most significant achievements. One result is this one young woman (my daughter) who is able to live life fully expressed without the weight of the shame, guilt, and embarrassment that abuse brings with it.

I don't consider myself an expert in any one particular area, although I have been called on numerous times to help young people in crisis. My greatest gifts are having a compassionate ear and a loving heart.

I am an ordinary woman who has faced some extraordinary circumstances— overcoming the triple A's: Abuse, Abortion, and Addiction. Because of that, I'm wiser and stronger; and, I'm on a mission to tell the truth to liberate women and girls who are dealing with the effects of trauma. I know from experience that the TRUTH really does set you free.

There was a time in my life when I was riddled with shame, guilt, and embarrassment and kept quiet about the traumatic experiences in my life. I kept quiet because I was taught that was the way to be. What went on behind closed doors stayed behind closed doors. At the tender age of nine, when my fragile body was sexually violated by my mother's boyfriend, I kept it to myself. Fraught with fear, I never said a word about it to anyone. During my youth, I also found out that my father and grandfather were one and the same person. It took nearly my entire lifetime to actually be able to share that truth. Have you ever experienced something so devastating that you just couldn't bring yourself to speak about it?

Well, for many years, I felt dirty, isolated, and invisible. To add insult to injury, my mother married my abuser and then without discussion, changed my last name to his (from Harden to Chavis). I still remember wanting my mother to see me, hear me, believe me, protect me, and choose me over HER MAN.

Publicly, I wore a mask to hide the pain but privately I suffered. The pain of my past hovered over me like a dark cloud, relentlessly refusing to let go. It silenced my voice, stole my joy, and kept me stuck in a state of constant fear. The fear of someone finding out the truth about me. The fear of someone finding out the truth about my family. The fear of failure and the persistent fear of rejection.

Have you ever found yourself silencing your own voice, when you know your voice needs to be heard? Well, it's your time right now. **It's time for you to reclaim the power of your voice and rise up. You are not alone!** You owe it to yourself and the children who are waiting for you to show up for them.

If you read my memoir, *When a Lie Becomes the Truth*, you know that my life is literally an open book. In my memoir, I share the gut-wrenching truth of who I am: the abuse, the lies, the deception and how I found out who my father was. I also share my journey to make peace with it all.

To some, my life's experiences may seem tragic, but for me I'd like to say that my life has had a meaningful texture. It is not so much because of what I've overcome but because of what I've learned along the way.

Because of the loss, lies, and piercing pain I have experienced, I've learned to appreciate my blessings so much more. From these I've learned empathy and compassion. I've learned humility because I had humble beginnings and no matter what tomorrow may bring, I'm grateful to have made it through yesterday. I've learned the power of NOW because tomorrow really isn't a guarantee and never will be. I've learned the power of LOVE.

At the end of this lifetime that's probably all, we'll remember. I'm not sure about anything else because no one has come back from the dead to tell me. However, I'm willing to stand on LOVE until I find out something different. I've learned the power of FORGIVENESS and the space it creates for real joy and peace of mind. I've learned the power of TRUTH and the freedom truth provides. I've learned the importance of keeping my word especially when it's hard because all we really own is our word.

I've learned the importance of showing up for myself and others. Showing up for myself was the toughest part for me to master, but now I see that when I take care of myself I'm more capable of taking care of my loved ones. It's like that old adage about the oxygen mask: **before helping someone else with their oxygen mask you've got to make sure to put yours on first.**

I've learned to appreciate the precious moments along life's journey. Loss is a persistent theme of life but so is LOVE. It took longer than I care to admit, for me to focus on the latter, but that's really been the biggest lesson of my life. Focus on love and keep the faith. Things will always work out one way or the other. The greatest determinant of the outcome is the measure of your faith. My greatest losses have enlarged my capacity to love.

You may wonder what I've lost, so I will share the short list: my innocence at age nine, my first child at age 13, my first apartment at age 21, my first husband at age 35, my father, and recently I lost my mother to COVID. But through it all, I kept believing that if I just didn't give up on my dreams, things would work out.

I didn't know how I would create a better life but I kept praying, "God, please look past my faults and bless my life." And, I remember hearing a small voice calling me forward to TRUST in a power greater than myself.

Do your part and infinite intelligence will handle the rest. All I knew was to stretch out by faith and let the miracles happen. Through life's journey, I came to know for sure the power of one voice, the power of one good decision, and the power of faith in something greater than myself.

How do tragedies transform into -triumph? Through faith and works.

"Faith without works is dead."-James 2:17

Even when I didn't know how I would create a better life for my daughter and myself, I had the desire. You've got to want to clean up your act, and clear the confusion and chaos, in order to create a better outcome. We don't get the life we deserve; we get the life we create. Belief comes before victory.

Ask the ultimate force of the universe for help. Even if you have no idea of how things will all work out, trust that they will, and do everything within your power along the way. Through focused determined effort, things will shift.

"Be bold, and mighty forces will come to your aide." -Basil King

Make a bold request and let universal intelligence work it out on your behalf. My best advice is to be kind to children, whether yours by birth or not. Show up for your children and always be present for them. Learn to listen with your heart and give yourself permission to cry for yourself and for them, as you search to find the power of your voice.

Forgive yourself for all the things you told yourself you would do but never did. And, remember it's never too late to get started. The power is in the present moment, so, seize the day and get to work.

To become a dynamic woman, develop faith in yourself and a power greater than yourself. Act on your faith because when you stretch out on faith miracles happen, your goals are achieved, your dreams come true, and the dynamic woman within emerges into the full expression of YOU.

~ Jackie V. Harden

This story is for "The Girls"

This story is for "All the Girls."

This is for all the girls who have survived LOSS—the loss of a loved one: a mother, a father, a sister, a brother, a husband, a child, any family member, or a dear friend.

It may also be the loss of a limb, a breast, or even the loss of a job, a career, or an entire business.

Yes, this is for All the Girls. We know the statistics, but we don't know all their stories.

So, I celebrate all the girls who found the courage to stay here—to stay here in the game of LIFE—even after the LOSS—even when it seemed like you would never win.

This is for All the Girls who didn't give up, but found the courage to stay in the game, even while hurting. Somehow you found the strength to keep dribbling the ball; limp and all, just to take another shot.

This is for the Girls, who gave it all they got.

This is for All the Girls who found the courage to become moms, whether by choice or by force. You brought forth LIFE.

This for All the Girls—the girls who give life to the game, and who gave their life for the game.

Without YOU, life would never be the same.

Jackie Harden is a best-selling author, a strategic life coach, and motivational speaker. She is also the owner and CEO of Life of Victory Enterprises (L.O.V.E), a coaching and consulting company. With more than 20 years of experience in Human Resource Management, she is currently an Employee Relations Officer for the Newark Board of Education. Over the past 30 years, Jackie has transformed her life from a struggling single mother to a six-figure professional and entrepreneur. Jackie is passionate about working with women and girls to help them transform internally so they can lead lives of integrity, authenticity, and unconditional love.

Jackie is a woman of faith who loves listening to music, dancing, and spending time with family.

For more information or to contact Jackie, please see below:

Website: www.jackieharden.com

Email: jackievharden@gmail.com

https://www.facebook.com/jackiehardenlifecoach

https://www.instagram.com/jackievharden

https://www.linkedin.com/in/jackievharden

Chapter 10

Why Society's Blueprint for
Success
Couldn't Make Me Happy
By Joi M. Ross

"**D**ynamic Woman, wow, is that ME?" That's what I asked when I was invited to join this amazing project and group of women. I looked up the word "dynamic": lively, active, self-motivated, vibrant, forceful. The woman I see when I look in the mirror today is all of those things. So yes! Among other things, you could say that I am ... dynamic. Business owner, international best-selling author, leader, life-long learner, curious, a facilitator of transformation, lover of God and people. I mostly see myself, however, as a woman constantly learning, growing, evolving, and intentional about fulfilling my God-given purpose. But that wasn't always the case.

Most people who know me may not know that there was a time when, as a result of societal constructs and following society's "blueprint for success," I suffered with depression and identity issues. There I stood one Saturday, in the bathroom of my suburban home, looking in the mirror thinking about my new car parked in the garage, my multiple six-figure (and growing!) business, the graduate degree that I completed with honors while working full-time, and all of the volunteer work that I had done over the years including serving on the Board of Directors for a local women's shelter and serving in various church ministries. And yet, I was grappling with these nagging questions. Is this all there is? Why do I feel so unfulfilled when I've checked so many boxes that are supposed to lead to "happy ever after"? I felt disillusioned, confused and honestly ... a bit guilty. How dare I feel this way when I had passed so many milestones that "on paper" put me in a category with a small percentage of women, minorities, and business owners? I didn't believe I had a right to feel unhappy given that I had so much, while so many people had far less.

You see, like many people in western society, I had fallen prey to the deception of fairy tales and movies that too often lead us to believe that if we work hard enough, get an education, land a great job or start a business, make "good" money, get married ... etc. ... we'll live happily ever after. Sounds good. But it's oh, soooo untrue! I stand now, so grateful for being awakened to the truth about fulfillment, joy, peace, and abundance. These things, contrary to what society often leads us to think, are an inside-out job. No external signs of "success", achievements or money can bring these things into our lives. The truth is, freedom, fulfillment, joy, peace and abundance, comes only through the disciplined work of going inward and upward. Put another way, as we begin the work of getting aligned spiritually with God and yielding to a process of heart and mind renewal, excavating beliefs and thought patterns that are contrary to our true identity, the "REAL US" begins to emerge.

I discovered that my true self could only be revealed in direct proportion to my willingness to develop a personal relationship with God. When I began an intense journey to learn about Him and His true character, I began to see the REAL ME that had been buried underneath society's rules and the false stories in my head. Underneath it all was untapped power and a purpose that was far beyond money, business, and material things.

This beautiful discovery came on the heels of what was both the best of times, and the worst of times – skyrocketing business success while my health and personal life were spiraling downward. That's when my transformation from the inside-out began.

There I sat in my luxury car, crying in the parking lot and feeling like someone was playing a cruel joke on me. You see, 15 minutes earlier, I had been in the doctor's office for what I thought would be a "routine" follow-up visit. The nurse had explained that my doctor was out but her partner was going to see me. It was odd they didn't tell me in advance that my doctor was out, but I figured "what the heck, let's get this over with." I had a client meeting to go to and just wanted to get my test results and leave. I was THAT girl ... driven, motivated, with no time for waiting in a doctor's office when I could be working and closing deals! I had just opened a new office, hired new staff, my schedule was busy, and my days were hectic. So there I sat, legs crossed, looking down at my new shoes and feeling confident about the presentation I'd be making later. I was visualizing myself in the room with my clients, when the door opened and this male doctor I had never seen before walked in ... without a smile. I recall trying to spark conversation and make small talk to get a smile out of him. He showed no personality. While looking down at my chart, instead of at me, he finally spoke and said "So, your test results are back ... it appears you have thyroid cancer." I felt numb, as if I had floated out of my body.

I began laughing out loud. I remember saying, "I'm so sorry for laughing, it sounded like you said CANCER! I must have misunderstood. What did you say?" He replied, "Yes, you have cancer." My emotions were numb and my logic kicked in. I began asking questions. I wanted to know all the scenarios ... worst case scenario, treatment options, what if I did nothing, can I get a second opinion, and so on. Then, I abruptly stood up, said "I have a meeting to get to" and proceeded to leave. Internally, I was thinking, WHAT? I don't even know how to process this! This can't be happening! How could this be real? Oh shoot! I really don't have time for this! I have to get to my meeting!

You see, on the outside, I was living the dream! I was checking all the boxes and doing most of the things on society's "blueprint for success." I was eating a mostly certified organic diet, running 4-5 times a week, working with a personal trainer, growing my business and keeping my clients happy. AND, I was a faithful church attender, believer in God, a generous giver. I wasn't perfect by any means, but I certainly was trying to do all the "right" things.

While the "signs of success" stacked up externally, internally I was feeling more and more unfulfilled, like something was off. At times, I felt like I was living someone else's life and there was a REAL me buried deep inside who desperately wanted to be set free. I tried to ignore those feelings because honestly, I was afraid of what might happen if I allowed myself to sit still and listen. I was afraid that my life would be uprooted. I tried to feel better by adding things to my life – people, shoes, clothes, luxury vacations, food, alcohol ... and other vices.

The more I reached outside of myself for things to make me feel better, the worse I felt and the louder that nagging internal voice became. It was saying "NO! Don't Settle! There IS more! You were meant for more!" I felt like the "real me" buried deep inside was screaming for me to save her life! But saving her would require me to make major changes. I would have to hit "pause" on my 90-mile per hour lifestyle, pull over on the side of the road, and have a serious come to Jesus meeting (as my parents used to say) with myself. It would require me to get very real and deeply honest; and that was scary!

I didn't know what I was going to do, but what I knew for sure was that I had to do something. Change was critical. I was convinced that my chronic, unaddressed stress and failure to listen to that internal voice had now led to health issues. I was not willing to continue down the path of following someone else's blueprint for success while literally killing myself in the process. No amount of money was worth that! So, I did the only thing I knew to do. I got on my knees and poured my heart out to God.With tear-filled eyes, I asked Him to help me; to give me wisdom and to instruct me on what steps to take. You see, I grew up in a pastor's family and had always had a foundation of spirituality and Christianity since childhood. But I had rejected "religious rules, do's and don'ts" in my 20s and embraced a "non-religious" view of Christianity focused on a personal relationship with Jesus. I had faith. I had seen the powerful results of prayer, and I knew, without a doubt, that God cared about me. I believed with all my heart that He wanted better for me. He had beautiful plans for me.

In my darkest moment, God met me where I was --- when I was facing a health crisis as well as an internal crisis of needing desperately to change my life but not knowing where to start. My transformation started with downloads and revelations about His deep love for me and His plan for my life. He showed me that the universe was designed to support me and bring me good things. He assured me that a bright, beautiful future was ahead. He told me that my current trials were temporary and that He is the God who heals, and He would certainly heal me! He spoke to me about things I thought were addictions, and explained those things were NOT in fact addictions. Rather, I was in bondage to my own limiting, self-critical thoughts and didn't even know it! FREEDOM was, in fact, my birthright! He had already set me free! I simply needed to believe it and see myself that way. Good things were lining up in the universe, hovering, waiting to come to me. Everything was waiting for ME to be awakened to the truth of my identity and purpose. These were some of the things I heard in those months of prayer, stillness, and listening for God's voice. This revelation changed me forever!

I stand today, completely healed, addiction-free, filled with purpose, loving who I am, self- employed and helping others to live their best lives – because my life has been transformed from the inside-out and I'm 100% rooted and grounded in my true identity. God's LOVE changed me! His presence inside of me causes me to prosper and bloom wherever I'm planted. And I am blessed to be a blessing. I truly believe that, only when we know the Creator's love for us can we truly know and love ourselves and understand our purpose in the world.

It brings me joy to help others discover their true identity, how to tap into the power within, and how to experience freedom, abundance and joy. Through my weekly radio show and podcast, Living Inside-Out Today with Joi Ross, as an author, through 1-on-1 and group coaching and training sessions, and other methods, I am on a mission to facilitate inside-out transformation in others. Why? Because joy, freedom, fulfillment and abundance are our God-given birthright!

Joi Ross is an international best-selling author, facilitator of change and personal transformation, lover of people, and CEO of APEX Direct, an award-winning communications consulting firm. She also hosts "Living Inside-Out Today," a weekly radio and podcast show.

As a result of working with APEX, clients more effectively communicate with empathy and impact. Clients hire Joi to create communication strategies and deliver training in areas such as, identifying and overcoming stereotypes and barriers to effective communication; community engagement; climate and environmental justice; and service excellence.

Under Joi Ross Consulting, a separate business entity, she focuses on writing, speaking, training and facilitating personal development and transformation. Her focus is helping people experience fulfillment, joy and freedom from limiting beliefs. Those who know her describe Joi as warm, kind, and down-to-earth.

Websites:

https://joiross.com

https://AlwaysPursuingExcellence.com

Social Media:
https://www.facebook.com/joi.ross.77
https://www.facebook.com/JoiRossConsulting/
https://www.instagram.com/JoiRossConsulting/
Podcast and Talk Show:
Living Inside-Out Today with Joi Ross
https://VoiceAmerica.com/show/4067 (Live on
Thursdays, 9aPacific)
Email: LivingInsideOutToday@gmail.com

Chapter 11

Awakening the Dynamic Woman in Me
By Twyla Stubblefield

I was born in northern Louisiana during segregation; a real, not-so-long-ago time, when being Black meant you were second class. This was a time when women, especially Black women, had a designated place and were expected to remain there. In America, in order to move up the social ladder, and to have more access to wealth and higher education was the key. Society had set the precedent that if you went to college, you could become an elite member of society.

Black women were still almost the exception to this general rule. For us, being barefoot and pregnant was the expectation. However, in my family, my parents believed in more. There were no limitations for us, no set lines drawn that we were not allowed to cross.

As educators, my mother and grandmother were the ones who established what our paths were to look like. The path was to finish high school without getting pregnant, go to college, get married, and then have babies. Not going to college was not an option. I was an obedient child and did what was expected. My dream after my education was to get married and live happily ever after.

In Black society then, married people stayed together no matter what. Religion has always played a significant role in establishing our standard of morality. This pitfall of thinking could create a foundation that could either become a blessing or a curse. The common saying those days was, "What goes on in the house stays in the house." Family matters were never to be discussed outside your four walls. That way of thinking inhibited a family from seeking counsel through therapy or even the counsel of relatives and elders. It locked families into a family unit that was not healthy and, in some cases, dangerous.

When you walked out your door, you had to put on a 'mask' and smile as if everything was wonderful. The title of Mrs. was supposed to be worn as a badge of honor. It was implied that your happiness directly correlated to your marital status. The picture to the world was: you were blessed and highly favored. Taking vows in front of God and your family was supposed to make life easy, right? Wrong! It didn't matter what was said in church;

women would be suffering and hiding the pain behind the masks and closed doors.

As I said before, I was extremely obedient. I took my parents' premade plan for my life and stepped into adulthood in search of a happily-ever-after life. I went into my marriage based on what I had witnessed to what marriages looked like from the outside. I watched my mother, grandmother and great aunts navigate seemingly happy marriages. I just assumed that I was going to be married, and be happy forever, just like they were.

That notion was short lived, as you obviously could conclude. You know what happens when you assume? I assumed that I knew what it took to have a strong, happy marriage. I assumed that we'd have little disagreements, but everything would just naturally work itself out. Ultimately, when things weren't going right, I thought to myself, What *happened? What am I doing wrong*? When times got very hard I thought to myself, *Mom, why didn't you tell me that things would happen and situations could become so unbearable?*

I think my biggest hope, looking back, would have been that my mom would have taught me how to navigate through disagreements and conflict. I wish I would have known how to say how I felt! I wanted to ask my grandmother, "Why didn't somebody sit me down and tell me what marriage really looked like? Why did you let me blindly walk into this?"

When I did look to my mother and grandmother for wisdom, I was told to pray, or stay; while the world felt like it was falling down around my feet. I realized that their mothers never taught them about marriage and what marriage was all about either. They could not give them the tools to keep a marriage healthy and full of love because they never had them to give.

Growing up, we never talked about how we felt beyond the surface. Emotional conversations were few and far between. I can just imagine that it was the same in other Black households as well. I had no understanding of how to handle disagreements, or how to tell my husband how I needed to be loved. I had no idea of how to meet his needs emotionally, how to build the bridge that would aid in connecting him to his emotions, or how he should articulate them to me. The examples I had showed me how to get married; not why I should get married, or how to stay married.

The time finally came when I realized that both of us had to work on our marriage together in order for things to change. There then came the time when I realized that it wasn't working, and that I needed to let go. I can remember when the light bulb came on: I was at a personal development conference and the facilitator was talking about, *Dreaming, and How to Create Your Life*. I wanted a life filled with peace. I wanted a partner who knew what he needed and who would give me what

I needed in return. I wanted someone in my corner who would fight for me and I for them. I had never had that in 29 years of marriage. Marriage is a contract that many of us never received the paperwork for.

After the conference, *What-ifs* began to invade my mind. I went back and forth still trying to figure out (by myself) how to make my marriage work but knowing in my heart that my husband had been emotionally disconnected, and I was not a priority in his life. He operated with the attitude; *I can do whatever I want because I am a man.* That made me realize that I was on my own. It was time for me to make a plan to move on. The dream that I had as a child of being married, having a big house, and living in the suburbs with the white picket fence just wasn't going to work out. There was not going to be a Cinderella story ending. I began to ask myself a few questions: "What do I do? Where do I go? How do I move on?"

After that awakening, I decided with a lot of uncertainty and unknowns, that I had to find the courage to create a different life. Looking back, I realize that I was at the beginning of becoming a dynamic woman. My failed marriage laid the foundation for a new start. I finally made a choice for myself to not live in silence or embarrassment anymore. **I decided to take off the mask**.

I had to learn to trust God to guide me through. I learned to exercise faith and action. I didn't know what my future would look like, but it had to be better than what I had settled for. It was the first time in my life that I made a conscious decision to get off the predetermined plan that had been handed down to me by my elders. Otherwise, I would still be married, coasting to the 40-year mark in pain, looking very poised and smiling like the Queen of England.

My new direction began by me being honest with myself; acknowledging that I had participated in the failure of my marriage because I was in no way ready for marriage. I was ill-equipped on so many levels. I took an assessment of my emotional and financial situation. I found a church that taught the Word of God without fanfare, but more importantly, I started to study the Word on my own. It was different when I read it for myself—The Word brought me peace.

The biggest change came in my life when I found Lisa Nichols: a mentor and a teacher. She opened up a new world that I didn't know existed. I then started to work on myself. I learned how to look at myself and learned to believe in myself. I also heavily invested in personal development. I read books that taught me how to express myself, and how to find peace after losing my marriage. I also learned how to write a brand-new roadmap for my life—one that I felt comfortable being the driver.

- A Dynamic woman is constantly seeking and actively pursuing the best version of herself. It's seeking guidance from God; it's realizing that there are people on this planet that have been in the same situations we find ourselves in.

- Dynamic women seek the counsel of wise people. With wise counsel, prayer, and creating goals, there is nothing a dynamic woman cannot achieve.

- Dynamic women make goals that are out of their comfort zones, and they seek out other people who force them to grow and achieve those goals. That group of people will be there to support them in achieving their goals. The beauty about growth is that you will start to find opportunities you didn't know you could have had, and things you never thought about doing will start to happen when you choose to create a new life.

- A dynamic woman realizes she has to work on herself. Pain, sadness, and isolation will create false internal narratives that could cause her to write untrue stories about who she really is. Those things could be conscious or unconscious and could hinder her from being who she really wants to be.

I choose to believe that I am that dynamic woman who, every day, is working to become even more empowered to leave a trail for other "delusional" women to follow.

Twyla Stubblefield is a former Principal Food Scientist at a fortune 500 Food and Beverage Company. Her new career is in the Real Estate Industry where she is a real estate investor who is building a platform to teach financial literacy to baby boomers. When she is not teaching, she enjoys growing vegetables in her urban garden. Twyla has two adult children. She lives in Louisiana.

For further information or to contact Twyla, see below:

Email: tstbblfld@gmail.com

Instagram: @twylastubblefield

Chapter 12

Dynamic Power
by Alana Apryl Major

Originating from the Greek word, dynamis, "force power", the energy of the word dynamic, fosters themes of action, progress, forces producing motion, new initiatives, positive ideas, periodic application of voltage, and my favorite: the potential to generate extreme reactions. Layering dynamic power at first glance would appear unvarying. On the contrary, however, noting the uniqueness of what is created and yielded from a woman, dynamic power is worthy of repeating.

Growing up I admired beautiful women, foremost, my mother. Strength of character, class, charisma, cheer, and some chaos meshed beautifully together embody her on a day-to-day basis. She taught me to identify the truth of beauty and thus I was awed at the lady sitting in the back of the church, inebriated with the Spirit, singing off tune as loud as she could— wearing delicate lace, freshly picked flowers and vibrant colours (too many to mention). She was expressing herself without reservation as she shared her heart with God. I admire her. I am awe at the precious lady who was consciously aware, resilient, and true, who stares back at me and through me.

I also admire beautiful strong women like Christina Fernandez de Kirchner, who grew up in a remote town, unknown and ignored, but caught the eye of a young ambitious man. She loved him, married him, bore his children, and supported him as he served his country. When destiny called him home, she took his place as President of their country.

The admiration of beauty observed creates this dynamic energy referred to inside of me, and the characterization of this dynamic power overflows and spills out in various expressions—mostly prose. The snippets provided here in this Dynamic Women Anthology showcase this and will knowingly or very quietly create the same energy in you as you embrace it.

As women, our purpose and blessing are so vast it may take an eternity for us to grasp it all. Pondering the women you know and admire helps you to realize how tremendous the full scope of being a woman is. Women hold many positions in friendship, family, community, and society: mothers and lovers, caregivers and nurturers, soothing souls and rambunctious warriors, sisters and soldiers, confidants and creators. Harnessing, yielding, and wielding illustrate that women are dynamic with dynamic power, and as we journey here my poetry intends to unveil this.

The beauty is that dynamic power is inherent. Whether realized or unrealized it is present and naturally exudes. Certainly, it is to everyone's benefit that as a young woman grows and develops, she is able to aptly learn of her dynamic power. Flourishing women are urged to wisely utilize it, and mature women gift it to future generations.

Tomorrow

Tomorrow does not exist;
For tomorrow upon arrival is kissed
With the newness of today;
Forgoing the past and embracing its stay.
Yesterday will never be;
For yesterday upon departure layered memories cast for us to see;
With the loss of yesterday,
We love and lend with knowing there is no tomorrow, yet capturing all of today.

You

Like the silent river steady flowing, all serene;
Breathing life into teams of fish and purifying all that was unclean.
Soothing its way along with pulses and cool flows;
Intentionally steering everything in the direction you want it to go.
Slowly making your way through, practically unnoticed;
Filled with life, purpose and intensely focused.
Captivating and glistening in the early morning light;
Mysteriously sparkling when the light leaves sight.
Transforming shorelines and transfixing rocks;
Catching broken leaves while dominating stalks.
You possess rare power, strong, gracious and true;
Bringing all to a waterfall end, that yields their beginning too.

Destiny

Destiny, like a cheetah pursuing its prey,
will in quiet and undetectable fashion,
observe and strategically await the precise moment to pounce,
and render you helpless to fate!

As I Blossom!

The wonder of the sunlight greets and awakens me in the morn
To life anew, inspired and newborn.
I am kissed softly and gently by falling dewdrops;
Embraced and caressed by tender breezes from my stem all the way to my top!
I am about to blossom!
It's amazing to gaze at the wonder about me;
Wonder, it seems no one but I can see.
I love the frenzied treasures and the frazzled frailties sprouting from the ground;
The delicate paws and hefty hoofs that dance about me... all around!
About to blossom!

I have grown and matured, and I am ready to meet them all,
It's now time for me to embrace my destiny, my call.
Time for me to add to the wonder of this world around me,
Time for my beauty that is wrapped within to be set free!
Wonders of the blossom!

My petals have shielded my precious and magnificent parts;

Protected my future seedlings from carelessness and destruction before their start.
My stem is strong and is the backbone to my wisdom and beauty;
My leaves are extended, graceful and are ready for any duty.
I blossom!

Here I go, fierce and wonderful world!
Cruel and tempting, rewarding and true!
Here I go, fierce and wonderful world!
I am about to give the love in me... to you!
I blossom! I am wild! I am graceful! I am an Orchid!

Alana Major was destined to be a gifted, eloquent, natural leader. Her developmental pursuits culminate with a Master of Business Administration degree in Healthcare Administration, numerous industry designations and recently heading one of the largest insurance companies in the Bahamas.

Her commitments yielded notable achievements including 2014/2015 President of the Year for the International Region of Alpha Kappa Alpha Sorority, Inc., Founding Director and President of One Blood Bahamas and in 2016, Leading Lady of the Bahamas.

Her evolution continues as an Entrepreneur, Head Consultant, PHA Director of Foundations, Author & Poet, Public Speaker & Motivator, TV/Radio Host and as a Woman on a mission fighting causes larger than herself whilst embracing change for the better.

For further information or to contact Alana, see below:

Email: alana_apryl@hotmail

Chapter 13

Breaking Free
By Lilian Okech

It was a beautiful day and all the children in my neighborhood came together under the "big tree" to play, 'Pretend Husband and Wife.' We girls chose our husbands and took care of the house as good wives. We built our houses with sticks and grass; used cans for cooking, and some old clothes for bedding. To us, it was a fun game to prepare us for our future.

When I was just 9 years old, I heard my mom calling me from a distance of about fifty feet from home. I hurriedly dropped the 'food' I was cooking for my pretend husband and ran in the direction of my mom's voice. Just before I got too close to her, she stopped me and said, "Go and call your sister, Regina."

"Oh ok", I said. I ran as fast as I could, to call my sister Regina. Regina is my first sister, who already had children. I found her, grounding sesame butter to make soup. "Mom is calling you," I said. She followed me back to our mother. Then mom said something to my sister that wasn't clear to me. My sister then turned to me and said, "Go back home!" I couldn't go back to playing anymore; all I could think about was what could be going on with my mother. I was curious, but I said nothing. I just went back home. When I was growing up, children were not allowed to question their seniors, especially their parents.

After a few minutes, my sister came home with something wrapped up in her arms. She called me over and said, "Look at your baby sister!"

"Wow!" I exclaimed. I was shocked when I realized what had happened. Our mom was having a baby right there in the garden! My sister saw my concerned face, and said "Mom is fine, she will come home soon." She then put the baby in bed and took mom some hot water.

I then realized how carefully and slowly mom walked. In fact, I realized how much smaller her stomach was then, which confirmed in my mind that Mommy was pregnant all that time. Women back then didn't speak much about being pregnant, childbirth, or birth control. We children just played with our baby siblings and helped to take care of them. As soon as girls turned five years old, our baby siblings were placed on our backs with a handmade baby-carrier wrap cloth.

Seeing how strong my mother was, encouraged me to be strong when I came to America. My mom was open-minded and wanted better for us. She knew if we had better opportunities, we could be anything in life.

I was fifteen years old when I came to America. It was January 19, 2005, a cold winter day. When we arrived from Uganda, it was me, my mother, and six of my siblings. We arrived in New York City, John F. Kennedy Airport with no jacket, open shoes, and T-shirts. To say we were freezing is an understatement.

Our caseworker met us at the airport. She was tall and beautiful, with light brown skin, and long thick black hair. I remember her wearing a long brown coat with black high-heeled boots, and she walked with confidence. She introduced herself to us and said she was from the United Nations Refugee Agency. When she looked over at me and asked my name, I remember feeling speechless. I looked away and thought, *Wow! I have never seen a woman like this before.*

I gazed around the vicinity, and noticed women from all nationalities. Many of them were dressed and looked like professionals; others were just ordinarily dressed. To me, they all appeared busy and yet seemed so free. I was in awe! I wanted to be like them: I wanted to be free, I wanted to do something of importance in life just like those confident women seemed to be doing. I could just taste it and feel it. My imagination took me away and I imagined myself wearing a long coat, dressed for business. I thought, *Yes, I am in America now and free to become anything I want to be!*

Just five years before, at age ten, I was a village girl who had never been to school. It was very embarrassing for me, but that was my reality. Being sickly as a child was one of the many different circumstances that prevented me from going to school.

Although our single mother had eight children, she did her best to put all of us through school, even though she had never been to school herself. Of course, she wanted us to break free from that 'disability'. America offered me something better, and I was determined to make use of the opportunity. I was excited!

Everyone seems to be looking for something greater than himself/herself. Why is that? Could it be the power of the human spirit that the Creator has given us to become better? Is it a plan that far exceeds what we can possibly imagine? Why is it that some people reach their highest potential and some don't? Is it because of the pressures of life that we sometimes become brainwashed and lose sight of what's really important—things to discover and to do?

When I came to America, I knew that I wanted to be something. I knew when I first arrived at the airport that day, that I was going to be a professional woman, just like my case worker. I could feel it in my spirit.

Well, instead of working on my desires and goals, I was forced to become a bride at the age of 16. The thought of marrying made me anxious and afraid, because I knew I wasn't ready to be a wife; I had so many dreams and goals.

Eventually, I did get married and had four children. The relationship was abusive and controlling, and after ten years I decided that the abuse had to stop. I decided to leave my husband, but the fear of the stigma I would face in my community made leaving difficult and complicated. In my culture, there is a certain expectation of marriage and family: divorce is taboo.

I sought help but most of the women were in similar situations as I, and therefore they could not help me. I did not have a degree: I had to make money to feed my children, so I started cleaning people's houses. This gave me a stable income and I was then able to take care of my children. When I saw how having a stable income helped me, I wanted to help other women who were in the same helpless situation that I was in; and that's how my business was born.

I started a cleaning company and hired women that were in the same situation as myself: helpless, and the sole provider for them and their children. Some of the women left everything and ran with only the clothes on their backs. They needed clothes, shelter, and furnishings. When I received donations of clothes and furniture from my new business partners, I recycled them into the hands of the victims; who eventually became my employees.

According to the World Health Organization (WHO) violence against women – particularly intimate partner violence and sexual violence – is a major public health problem, and a violation of women's human rights. Estimates published by WHO indicate that globally about 1 in 3 women have been subjected to either physical and/or sexual intimate partner violence or non-partner sexual violence in their lifetime. Worldwide, almost one-third of women aged 15-49 years, have been in intimate partner violence relationships. These have reported that they have been subjected to some form of physical and/or sexual violence by their intimate partner.

Sadly, I was one of those women. And I've had people ask me, "How could you be in a relationship like that and keep having children?" *How could I answer a question like that?* All I can say today is this, *I didn't have the knowledge at the time because I was a child myself, having children.*

We are the sum of our environment and what we learn. When we have come to know better, we are supposed to do better. We should always be our best selves no matter where we find ourselves. Take for example my strong mother back in Africa: although she did not go to school, she has a natural gift when it comes to keeping a good household and taking care of her family. She was the first child of my grandfather's second wife and was treated unfairly, yet she loved creating a happy home for her family.

I chose to be happy and think differently as I now understand that I am a dynamic woman. That child bride became a woman, and that woman became unstoppable. I hope you will understand that you too are a dynamic woman despite what you've been through. No matter where you start from, develop a growth mindset and believe that your Creator has a purpose for you.

Quoting from the Bible: Matthew 22:36-40 (NIV) One of the experts of the law asked: "Teacher, which is the greatest commandment in the law?" Jesus replied, "Love the Lord your God with all your heart and with all your soul and with all your mind. This is the first and greatest commandment. And the second is like it: Love your neighbor as **yourself**. All the Law and the Prophets hang on these two commandments."

My Commitment to Loving Myself

1.   One of the most important things to remember in the pursuit of life is that it is okay to be single. Never be okay with being entangled!
2.   Singleness (Individuality) is the foundation of all relationships.
3.   Singleness determines the quality of all relationships.

4. The most important relationship in life is not interpersonal but an **intrapersonal** relationship. How we speak to ourselves.

Self-Love is a result of:

- SELF-DISCOVERY
- SELF-SOURCE
- SELF-WORTH
- SELF-ESTEEM
- SELF-CONCEPT
- SELF-IDENTITY
- SELF-VALUE
- SELF-CONFIDENCE
- SELF-RESPECT
- SELF-FORGIVING

So, my queens, if you want to be a dynamic woman, **take charge of your life first and then dominate.**

 **Lilian Okech** is a motivational speaker, entrepreneur, author, teacher, visionary and collaborative author with two Amazon number one bestselling books.

She is also the co-founder of Brother Tech Community Organization, an internet-café, and Computer Training center. This center brings Internet Services and computer training closer to people of South Sudan.

Her goal is to help build internet cafés for local schools to help the population increase their knowledge with computers, the internet, and computer training. This will help the population connect to the World Wide Web.

Her goal is to change South Sudan in the advancement of technology and motivate younger women and men to pursue their goals.

To contact Lilian, please see below:
Website: https://lilianokech.com/
Email: Lilian@LilianOkech.Com

Chapter 14

You Are Your Lifeguard
By Anastarcia Palacious

I live in The Bahamas. It's an archipelagic nation, meaning that there are multiple islands that make one nation. One of those islands that I love to visit frequently is the island of Eleuthera. The ocean side and seaside are as different as can be, with one featuring monstrous waves and the other a soothing calm. On both sides are stunning beaches. I was walking along one of these beaches, when I saw a sign that read "No Lifeguard on Duty, swim at your own risk." Now, this resort is on the Atlantic Ocean side, so while the beach is beautiful and the sunsets are amazing, on the calmest days, the waves coming into the shore banks kiss your cheeks aggressively. You must be confident to get into that water. You must be willing to embrace the feeling of wet sand between your toes and the inexplicable peace that washes over you as the waves continue, unbothered to their destination. You must have more faith than fear because there is no lifeguard on duty. That sign took me back to the summer of 1995.

My parents both worked when I was small. We lived on the island of Grand Bahama while my grandparents and most of my aunts and uncles lived in New Providence. That meant there weren't any built-in babysitters. Most summers we were shipped off to spend time with family members but for some reason, this one summer we were in Freeport, Grand Bahama. My mom had heard about a summer camp at some church where the fees could fit our meager budget. My sister and I were enrolled the next day.

I didn't enjoy that camp. I get vague splashes of it in my mind, and can't pinpoint what happened there, but I know for sure that I didn't like it. I remember begging not to go back, until I learned that we would be going to the YMCA to swim on the last day. I looked forward to that day with anticipation. I laid out my swimsuit the night before. I pretended to swim standing up. I was so excited! You see, my best friend Caitlin would go to Camp Curly Tail at the YMCA each summer, but my parents couldn't afford it; it was never an option. In addition to being allowed to go into the pool, I was also pleased to just be at the YMCA.

The day dawned with clear skies. We were loaded into buses and driven to the "Y." We lined up eagerly in swimsuits and with towels and goggles and swim caps. I didn't see Caitlin. They divided my age group into three more groups, those who had never swam before, those who could "manage" and those who were expert swimmers with lessons. To this day I'm not sure why in the world I thought going into the middle group made sense for me, but I chose my destiny. I was given a blue kickboard and waited patiently in line for my turn.

The objective was simple: I was to jump into the pool with the board and swim to the coach waiting on the other side. The whistle blew and I was in there like swimwear, making my way across the crowded pool to the coach on the other side who just happened to be talking to another youth counsellor at that exact moment. The pool was shaped like a giant L with a group of a dozen children clustered around various corners. I could see at least two groups of students and the coach I was swimming toward when suddenly, everything went blue.

I was under the water and there was something, rather someone, weighing me down. I couldn't make sense of what was happening, all I knew was that I couldn't breathe; I fought with everything in me to break the surface of the water.

"H-e-l-ppp–" I couldn't even get the word "help" out before I was dragged down again. The weight was another little boy. He wanted my kickboard, and he was doing whatever it took to push himself up, by pulling me down. I can't tell you what my seven-year-old brain was thinking but I somehow made it above water and again screamed for the three seconds I could see above the pool "Helppppp!" Down I went again—unable to breathe—completely terrified—just needing air. On and on it went: he pulling me down—I clawing my way back up; until finally, someone spotted us and rescued us out of the water. I don't remember who came to our rescue.

My understanding of the whole incident later was that the boy jumped in, got scared and reached out for the first thing he could hold on to; and that just happened to have been me. No one who should have been watching saw until it was almost too late. **There was no lifeguard on duty.**

Dynamic women, in our own lives we must recognize that we are the only lifeguards on duty. We must be the ones to advocate for, push for, and fight for our lives. When we are willing to cry out for help and battle everything sent to drag us down, the help will come, but it starts with us.

Many years later, I was emotionally drowning in a pit of purposelessness. I had the right people around me: my husband, a baby girl who had just celebrated her birthday, and the most profitable contract my new business had ever seen. Just like that day at the "Y", the conditions were perfect and yet the weight of meaninglessness threatened to drown me. We all have moments, days, and sometimes what feels like years of trauma that are intent on weighing us down. We can give in to the pressure and let our dreams die, or we can claw our way back to the surface long enough to yell for help.

I cried out for help through prayer. I was raised Christian, and faith is an important part of my life. I prayed earnestly to God for the tools and resources to achieve the purpose I felt he'd put in my heart. Many of us know the thing we've been called to do, but few of us have access to the tools or even fully understand the skill sets necessary to get us there. I prayed feverishly, and as He always does, God answered spectacularly. The funny thing about answers to prayers is that they are in the making long before we realize they are happening. In that instance, it was a bold step that I took to answer an invitation that would lead me down the path to catapulting my purpose.

I got a call one random afternoon with an offer to do a TEDx talk in my hometown of Freeport, Grand Bahama. I've been a speaker all my life, but this talk wrecked me. I debated calling it quits but as I proved in the water that day when I was seven—I'm a fighter. On the day of the talk, the participants and organizers gathered for a brief run-through. I still didn't have my speech together! I pushed my nervousness aside and embraced the moment to chat with the other speakers. That is how I met Caline Newton who was bringing Lisa Nichols to Freeport. She asked me about bringing Lisa on to a TV show that I host, and I agreed. Several weeks later, I boldly asked her if I could host a joint event with her in Nassau, and she agreed.

In a session filled with vulnerability, I spoke up and told Lisa about my frustrations. She invited me to join her at an event that she was having in just three weeks. I boldly said, YES and acted by investing in her weekend event. At that conference, I met phenomenal men and women whose lives and businesses opened my mind to another level of possibility. With Lisa's coaching and the backing of my community, I've watched myself swim safely to the other side. I fought for myself, and in doing so found a tribe willing to help me get out of the pool of purposelessness.

I don't know where you have found yourself in your journey as you read this. Maybe you are trying to impress or keep up with friends like I was that day at the "Y". Maybe you've jumped into something you've dreamed of and suddenly you get scared like the boy who jumped on to me and started to self-sabotage. Maybe it's the opinions of others holding you so far beneath the surface of your potential that you can't breathe. I can only imagine based on my own pools of doubt and despair, the challenges you've faced or the scars you are still bearing from the battles left behind. I can imagine that you are tired of always having to fight, but I encourage you to claw your way through one more time! Let me remind you that you are still here and in so being, there is more goodness to be found. There is no lifeguard on duty, but **you have you** and with a little bit of faith and a whole lot of fierceness, there is no pool you cannot swim out of, and no wave that can pull you under. **You got this!**

Anastarcia Palacious is the author of, A to Z to The Best Me, a television host, transformational speaker, and media coach. Anastarcia has over 70,000 hours of public speaking experience and has filmed over 750 episodes of live TV in the past five years. As a master storyteller, she has coached over 340 international business leaders in 43 countries on-camera confidence, public speaking, and style.

Anastarcia is a well-known facilitator, having traveled around the world to moderate events for various organizations. She has been nominated for and won various awards. She is listed on the Grand Bahama Wall of Fame. Anastarcia is married with two children.

To learn more about Anastarcia:

Website: www.homeofstars.com

Anastarcia@homeofstars.com

Instagram: @homeofstars

Chapter 15

She Speaks
by Prof. Joy Onyesoh

When my sister and friend, Dr. Denise Nicholson extended the invitation for me to join in this wonderful, inspiring project, I jumped on board because it was yet another opportunity to speak.

What is it about speaking that I love? Speaking is a way of revealing or unfolding my message to the world. It involves conscious and very intentional messaging, focused on creating impact and transformation.

We all have something to speak about and most times we are speaking in more ways than we realize. One of the distinguishing characteristics of a dynamic woman is her ability in speaking to make a difference. She doesn't just speak; she speaks intentionally—to strike a chord.

Now, the question may be, who is a dynamic woman? How can I become a dynamic woman who will be able to speak to make a difference? I would reflectively respond to these questions based on my life experiences.

Who is a dynamic woman?

I want to start off by looking at the word "dynamic". It is important to unpack it so we can explore the elements of the word.

Dynamic, as a noun is defined as a force that stimulates change or progress within a system or process. As an adjective, the word dynamic is defined in two ways – in relation to process or system, it is characterized by constant change, activity, or progress; while in relation to a person, it is being positive in attitude and full of energy and new ideas. I find both descriptions/definitions interesting and revealing.

Who is a dynamic woman? To answer this question, I will share a story with you, while you reflect. Let me take you back to a point in time in my life when I didn't fully know who I was, and didn't understand the fact that I was speaking consciously or unconsciously. I had a lot of energy to challenge the status quo, was optimistic in nature, and was willing to explore life to have a better understanding.

Growing up as a young girl in my clime—Nigeria, was one of the most rewarding and frustrating processes I ever encountered. Does it seem paradoxical that a process can be rewarding and at the same time frustrating? Yes,

I know it sounds weird but just join me on this reflective or throwback journey.

While in college, some of my coursemates took pride in being called *madam,* a term used to describe married female coursemates. For some reason, I can't place my fingers on it. I wasn't tripped to become a *madam.* In fact, I kept wondering how they arrived at the decision to get married while in school. I felt deep inside that there was more to life, and was determined to find meaning. I didn't realize that my curious and open mind would be the powerhouse that was driving most of my actions to date. Due to my convictions I made a decision not to get married until I was sure of what I wanted, and had an understanding of what the future held in store. The experience of watching the lifestyle of my coursemates, partly shaped some of my understanding of marriage and the need to be independent. It raised some critical questions in my young mind: questions such as, who am I? and what are my priorities in life?

One of the skills I have developed over time is the power of self-reflecting. I usually would play back experiences and reflect on my response or decision to self-validate. I would ruminate over whether I made the best decision at that time based on the available resources. I also noted if there were lessons to be learned from the situation. Since I have developed the skill set of doing this, I rarely over flog myself. I note where there are gaps, what I could have done better, and then move on. This is one way I keep my positive vibes on. To create change, you need to know how to self-validate and keep your momentum, because trust me, life will throw a lot at you.

I also learned how to give up my "perfectionist" syndrome. Now that I think about it, I can laugh, but trust me, this was a real challenge. I would want to do all the tasks myself; I wasn't satisfied when others did it their way, and that created a lot of anxiety. I eventually came to realize that there were several ways to get a task accomplished and that it was okay not to have a perfect outcome. This however, does not mean that attention to detail should be compromised.

When I had my first child, I practiced exclusive breastfeeding for three months before introducing milk. I wouldn't let anyone help with washing or sterilizing the bottles until I realized that it wasn't feasible to do everything myself while still working. I had my mom, who had come to stay with me. She came to give me support and help in caring for my baby. All I needed to do was to show her how I like it done. By the time I was on baby number two, my mom was completely responsible for the bottle care, while I checked in periodically to assure myself that my standards were being kept. This process deepened my understanding of delegated responsibility. A dynamic woman knows that she can't do it all and would never be scared or ashamed to ask for help, so that she can concentrate on other tasks that she can do so well. This process gets more tasks accomplished, and faster as well.

Understanding what your priorities are keeps you focused on what you need to get done. While I was in college, my priorities were to discover myself and go for my postgraduate studies. The understanding of this kept me going and I was able to register for some postgraduate degrees in a quick session. By the time marriage came, I knew I was ready to travel that path.

It is possible to become a dynamic woman at any point in life. One of the important aspects of becoming a dynamic woman is to recognize the agency that you possess. You also need to stay committed to your journey.

How to become a dynamic woman

There is no one way to become a dynamic woman, and I say this from my experiences and relations with other sisters. Every woman has her own perspective which is shaped by the way she has experienced the world. We have all come through different paths, but we understand who a dynamic woman is because we are the embodiments of dynamic women. To become a dynamic woman, there are some things that make you unique and you need to bring them fully to the forefront. It is important for you to commit to growth while honing and improving yourself on your life journey.

Seven Characteristics of a Dynamic Woman

Below are seven characteristics that you need to be intentional about if you want to become a dynamic woman:

#1. Experiences

One of the greatest influences in shaping an individual is her experiences. Our experiences determine how we show up and interact within the world. For instance, when a woman experiences a healthy relationship with her father, most times it makes her more trusting, self-confident, and willing to explore mutually beneficial relationships with her spouse. It doesn't mean that this is the norm for all women, however. Positive and negative experiences help us to understand the world better. They also help us understand how best to pursue a fulfilling life. Therefore be intentional about using your experiences; good and bad to help you become a dynamic woman.

#2. Passion

Passion is the feeling that drives us to become changed agents. It determines how we show up and provides the experience that allows us to create our unique impact in society. Understanding your passion is one characteristic of a dynamic woman. Your passion is like a divine call that helps you to know that you are uniquely positioned to be more, and it propels you to go forward, onward, and upward. It also helps your contribution to society.

#3. Personality

Your personality is uniquely your own and guides you in your life journey. This is what makes you who you are, and no one else can respond to your experiences with the same emotions, actions, and thoughts as you. Your personality is the combination of your qualities that form your distinctive character.

#4. Attitude

Your attitude is often shaped by your experiences and emotional state. Your attitude pilots how you perceive life and the actions of people around you. There are negative and positive attitudes, and these will affect your relationships with the world and the people who are in your circle. Your attitude is integral to living a successful and satisfying life. To live a satisfied and abundant life, you need a positive perspective. Your mindset must be able to possess a certain level of positivity and realism. Please take note that attitudes can be learned and unlearned.

#5. Perspectives

A person's perspective is uniquely his/hers. This is how one sees the world; it is one's point of view or way of regarding situations, facts, and judging one's relative importance. I often like to talk about, 'a silver lining in every dark cloud'; this is a perspective. It is my way of looking for opportunities and lessons in challenging situations. This has helped me to overcome a lot of barriers. A balanced perspective helps you to organize your thoughts and actions and make effective decisions. As a dynamic woman, you should remain open and ready to listen to another perspective.

#6. Goals

Your goals help to keep you focused and give a sense of the direction that your life is taking. It also connects you to your innermost desires and helps you to fulfill your purpose. Your goals speak about your personality, values, and passion.

#7. Spirituality

As a woman of faith, spirituality for me is at the center of all my life endeavors. Spirituality gives meaning to life and is based on choice and growth in knowledge. It helps one to become a better person and keeps one's hope alive. Spirituality also offers opportunities for relieving stress and finding inner peace. Some of the ways I practice my spirituality are by meditation, reading the Bible, listening to gospel music, and worship.

A dynamic woman speaks consciously and unconsciously through the exhibition of the characteristics listed above and more. Energy grows where focus goes; so be mindful of where you are investing your time, energy, and efforts; as these influence what you give and take from the world. You speak to make a difference, so speak intentionally Dynamic Woman, and change your world.

Prof. Joy Onyesoh is a Breakthrough and Transformative Leadership coach. She helps passion driven women identify limiting beliefs and roadblocks, and works with them to strategize action steps they can take to break through to the next level of their lives. She leverages on her personal transformative journey, over twenty three years experience working with women from diverse philosophical background , over a decade professional experience in transformative leadership and coaching experience to help women unleash their full potentials, achieve peak performance and live a life of abundance.

Joy is an alumnus of the California Institute of Integral Studies San Francisco California , Golda Meir

MASHAV Carmel international Training Center Israel and the Women's Human Rights Institute, University of Toronto Canada, a Rotarian and Paul Harris Fellow of Rotary International.

To contact Joy Onyesoh, please see below:
Website: www.joyonyesoh.com
Email: joyonyesoh@joyonyesoh.com
Facebook: joy Onyesoh
Linkedin: Joy Onyesoh PhD

Chapter 16

Regeneration of A Dynamic Woman
By Darnell Osborne

M y name is Darnell Osborne and I was born in 1967 in Nassau, Bahamas; the same year that The Bahamas achieved Majority Rule from Great Britain. Prior to my generation, women in Bahamian families either never received a formal education, or received a very abbreviated one. Our ancestors worked for survival and could only dream of a different future for their children. The daily routine of fishing, farming, and tending to household chores absorbed their time, and church attendance dominated the other waking moments. Those who were fortunate to secure the gifts of reading, writing or arithmetic were labelled, "smart".

My mother, Sybil Toote was born in 1945 in Nassau, Bahamas and was one of those blessed to be labelled as "smart". Whenever it was discovered whose daughter I was, and what profession I had followed—Certified Public Accountant, I was always told that my mom was brilliant in Mathematics.

Dynamic women are purposeful, honest, courageous, resilient, and confident. Women, no matter the disappointments in life, who get back up and try again, even if with tear-filled eyes. These are women who choose contentment instead of misery and sorrow; women who choose hope; and are not afraid to be honest and forthright.

My mother immediately comes to mind when I think of a dynamic woman. Mom (as she was affectionately called by all), suddenly found the rug pulled from under her when after 15 years of marriage, my father left the family and relocated abroad. Mom, with no husband and two teenagers to continue raising, found herself in a quandary. She was unemployed, with only basic education and no income. There were many days when Mom cried, but she grew stronger every day and most importantly, she never lost her joy. Mom was a woman of immense integrity, incomparable generosity, and simple decency. That was the legacy she left to her children.

Throughout my life I've experienced my fair share of joys and setbacks from which I have had to overcome and bounce back. For example, in April 2018, my beloved mother passed after a long chronic illness.

While I was still reeling from the loss of my mother, I was drawn into a very public controversy that attacked my character and threatened to ruin my personal and professional reputation. The toll it took on me was near devastating, especially because it was occurring close to Mom's death. This is where I had to rely on my sensible upbringing in order to maintain my psychological health.

Along the way, I have developed five principles that have guided me through tough times and empowered me to adapt, come out stronger, and transform into the dynamic woman that I am today.

These principles are:

1) Treat everything as a learning experience.

2) It is okay to take things day by day.

3) Give up the need to be liked and be prepared to stand alone.

4) Do not lose your moral compass.

5) Importance of sisterhood and learning to differentiate relationships.

Treat Everything As A Learning Experience

A dynamic woman learns to seek out the lessons in life. I have tried to find the lessons in even the toughest situations. One important lesson which I learned and which has aided in my development as a dynamic woman, is the value of one's character and reputation.

Had it not been for the qualities that I had spent a whole life and career-building, the outcome on my reputation from the very public scandal would have been even more destructive.

My first thoughts turned to what Mom had endured and her having to embrace new opportunities. I then started to see the silver lining in the dark cloud. I saw an opportunity to withdraw from public life, grieve Mom's death privately and to focus on personal interests. I developed a deeper relationship with my children and I was able to support their growth and development even more.

It is Okay To Take Things Day By Day

During those dark days after my mother's death and in the midst of the scandal, I had to learn to take things day by day. Some days I woke up and went right back to bed not wanting to face the realities of life. Other days, I spent hours praying, meditating, and listening to gospel or inspirational music to start my day off and pull me through the day.

As time went by, my ability to cope became easier. I learned to accept that some days would be better than other days. Each day is a gift—a blessing of time. I now embrace each day with a sense of purpose.

Give Up The Need To Be Liked and Be Prepared to Stand Alone

I was fortunate to develop independence over the years. As a dynamic woman, I learned to give up the need to be liked. As a leader, I have had to make hard decisions that were not popular, but that I believe were the right thing to do for the betterment of people in the long run. Oftentimes, people said I was foolish, but I remained focused on the bigger picture.

Once I pray, search my heart and soul, and feel deep down that it is the right decision to make, I then choose to lean forward without seeking approval for my actions through popularity. I never let the fear of failure overpower me and keep me from pursuing my aspirations.

The lyrics contained in one of my favourite gospel songs is, "Sometimes you have to encourage yourself;" and as dynamic women, this is what we have to do at times. Dynamic women believe that there is always a brighter day. We do not have control over the timing, but we believe and hope in the promises of God... that those situations will not remain the same forever. Sometimes people may have good intentions, but human beings are mere mortals. When I make a decision I know that it's God and Me... in me, around me, beside me, and more God than me.

Do not Lose Your Moral Compass!

Perhaps the greatest lesson that I have learned in life as a dynamic woman is the value of sticking to principles and the truth, no matter the cost. Although lies and mistruths may permeate the air initially, the truth will always set you free. People will question you and sometimes even your close friends or family members will doubt your decisions and not support your position. This is when you must remember that their resistance or objection may be based on their own insecurities, and their need to be liked or accepted personally or professionally. Hold fast to your moral compass and convictions. Never compromise your integrity or standards for short-term gain, to survive in a corrupt system.

Importance of Sisterhood and Learning to Differentiate Relationships

As a dynamic woman, I have learned the importance of having a group of other dynamic women to lean on. I have found it beneficial to surround myself with a handful of close friends; "sisters" who could provide encouragement and support on the days I feel most discouraged. Having built lasting friendships from childhood, there have been a small number of sisters who checked on me daily at my most vulnerable times. These relationships built over many years proved invaluable. In addition to these enduring friends, I was also introduced to a new community of dynamic women during the most trying time of my life.

I truly learned to appreciate the value of sisterhood in a community of like-minded women. There is a certain solace in knowing that you have access to dynamic women 24/7 who if needed, you can speak to without judgement and with understanding, and most importantly with prayer.

In conclusion: dynamic women have the ability to lead with power and courage. Power is the ability to have a vision and move towards it even when others don't see it. Courage is the ability to stand alone and move towards achieving your goals even when others don't support you. Dynamic women recognize their purpose—the reason why they are here on this Earth. Even when everything around her is not supportive, when everything around her is crumbling, when there is no light, when her good name is being slandered, when everything looks dark; in those moments, a dynamic woman relies on the principles and legacy that were left to her by her mother: which is to stand in her **integrity** and her **power**, and to have the **courage** to move forward with **grace** and always in **light**.

With positivity of thought, determination of spirit, truth in convictions, with support of her children, genuine friends, and the inspiration from her mother's life example; **I am that dynamic woman! I am my mother's child!**

Darnell Osborne is a Certified Public Accountant licensed under the Georgia State Board of Accountancy and is a member of the American Institute of Certified Public Accountants. She is also a licensed Chartered Accountant under the Bahamas Institute of Chartered Accountants (BICA) and an Accredited Director of the Chartered Governance Institute of Canada. She was elected President of BICA from 2014 to 2017.

Darnell has vast experience in the Financial Services Industry in The Bahamas. She was appointed as the first female Chairman of Bahamas Power and Light in 2017.

Darnell is an owner and director of the Dairy Queen franchise, operating in The Bahamas for the past 15 years.

Darnell is the founder of Citadel Consultants Ltd., a financial services consulting company. Darnell enjoys fostering Women's Empowerment.

Her website: http://www.citadelconsultantsltd.com
Website: https://darnellosborne.com/

Chapter 17

Dear Haiti, I am… Because of You
By Danita Sajous

It was a hazy, hot and humid day in June 1971. I was at the JFK Airport, in New York City. My bangs were stuck to my forehead as I boarded the 747 aircraft: this time, I was flying alone. I was equipped with my name tag, and passport neatly gathered in a pouch that hung around my neck. I sat in row 2A with my flight attendant, Alice, who was my escort. Back in the 70s children could travel alone—I was eight years old.

I was on my way to Port-au-Prince, Haiti. See, my dad is Haitian. At 25 years old he came to the United States with $500 in his pocket and a carry-on suitcase—a true immigrant, chasing the American dream. My mom was an American who embraced the Haitian culture. She spoke the language, cooked the food and created the first

Haitian-English Bilingual educational program in New York City. It was my turn to embrace my roots.

I was excited and nervous, but I knew I was safe because my uncle Bob would be at the Toussaint Louverture International Airport to pick me up. Bob wasn't really my uncle, he was my dad's best friend; and when he came to the USA, I would give up my bedroom so he would be comfortable. He was like a second dad to me.

My heart was racing with excitement and anticipation as we landed on the tarmac in Port-au-Prince. As I exited the plane, there was a hot breeze, a fragrance of burning wood, and the rhythmic sounds of Kompa music in the distance. Alice held my hand and off we went. I knew I was safe because I could see my uncle in the distance as my flight attendant escorted me through customs.

I ran up to my Uncle Bob, embraced him and held him tight. Uncle Bob packed my suitcase in the Jeep and off we went to my dad's hometown of Gonaives, a little suburb city in northern Haiti. I remember the white Jeep so well: it reminded me of the safari jeeps on the 1970's show, "Wild Kingdom"

Bubbling with excitement, I asked our chauffeur, how long was the ride, and he said that it was maybe about five or six hours. Back then, in 1971 Haiti didn't have paved roads. As we traveled the bumpy journey I could feel the heat on my forehead as I pressed my face against the back passenger window. I didn't want to miss a thing. Large woven baskets filled with lettuce, tomatoes, and carrots stood on the tops of women's heads, as they walked barefoot with rhythmic switches to their hips. As the jeep slowed down for an enormous pothole, I could see mud huts with thatched roofs. I found myself continuously waving back at all the children waving at me. Some had clothes on and some didn't. Some had shoes but most didn't. I watched families doing laundry in the river, and children laid their clothes on rocks to be dried by the midday sun.

Every once in a while our jeep would come to a complete stop! I'd lean over to the middle console to peer through the windshield. At one stop I saw a powerful river of muddy waters crossing our path. The river had overflowed its banks. The locals yelled to our driver and pointed to the area which was the shallowest. I could feel my heartbeat increase as the muddy waters came up to the base of my window and water entered the floor of the jeep. I felt like I was in a sinking boat ... We made it!! ... by God's grace ... we made it!

When we arrived it was pitch black. The jeep pulled up to the house full of mud. That Jeep that was once white was then brown. As we entered the gate, I heard dogs barking. As I plopped out of the jeep I felt teeth around my ankles. It didn't hurt though: It was my uncle's dogs Zoom and Tommy who appeared to be anxiously waiting to greet me with little love bites. Good thing I wasn't afraid of dogs.

I greeted the family that was awaiting our arrival. I was escorted to my room and my eyes got big with excitement. *Wow! A princess castle,* I thought to myself. There was a mosquito net over my bed. It was way prettier than the homemade castle that I would create with a green sheet draped over my Mom's sewing table—The perfect castle.

The next morning I woke up to roosters crowing and doves cooing. I didn't know how to speak Haitian Creole, but I quickly realized that I didn't need a language to communicate. We had a pool at our house, so all the kids (cousins) came to our house to swim and play. In the afternoon we'd go up the road to my cousin's house, and swim in the freshwater river behind their house. We'd jump off trees into the river, eat mangoes, and then the service maids would cook us beignets (banana fritters) sprinkled with sugar on top, which was for a penny each. *Awww, I can smell and taste them now, they were so good!.*

Learning Haitian Creole, was like a dance to me, and I got the rhythm. "Sak pase?" (what's up) Response: "N'ap boule" (we're burning - but it actually means "we're hanging out". Within two months, I was fluent. You see, when you're eight years old, your brain is like a sponge for languages.

When I heard the rhythmic sounds of "Pistache, Pistache, Pistache" (Peanuts, Peanuts, Peanuts) I knew it was market day! The road outside my window was bustling with activity. The women trudged for hours coming down the mountains with big baskets on their heads, heading to the marketplace to sell their goods.

There were no tents, no tables—just a dirt platform. It was like a scene out of Africa. Women with their colorful dresses squatted because there were no chairs. Some merchants brought their children ...I would get lost in the marketplace playing with them some days.

In Haiti, you either have money, or you don't. There's no middle class. I didn't understand that concept ... Everyone was human to me. I was often found in the maids' quarters playing with their young children.

Haiti was the world's first independent Caribbean state in the early 19th century. This was part of my rich and unique culture and it all fascinated me. I went back to Haiti every year until I was 14 years old.

At the age of 16, I spent my summer in Paris with a French family, who owned a small boutique hotel in the center of Paris. That was another time in my life that helped to cement my culture and I was excited to experience it. There in Paris, I stayed at the Hotel Boulevard. The owners were friends of the family and they welcomed me. I fit right in and continued to learn more about my culture. I enjoyed it all: from the trips to the baguette bakery across the street to a road trip through the South of France: Mariselle, St. Tropez, Cannes, Monaco, and Nice.

The aroma of both Haiti and France is me: the taste of the food, and every sound that comes from the belly of Haiti is me. From the women heading to the market with songs to the bongos, and their melodious sounds that move me involuntarily, all the way down to the roosters and doves that woke me up in the mornings—It is all a part of me.

My extended family is what I like to call a "mixed cocktail". We are Haitian, Chinese, German, Italian, and Swedish. This background enables me to believe in humanity and embrace my roots.

I am a dynamic woman because of my rich cultural background... The background that goes with me in every room and introduces itself as soon as I say my name— Danita Sajous.

You are a dynamic woman because of your experience, culture, trials, and your triumph.

My Haitian experience...makes me a dynamic woman.

My parent's sacrifice... makes me a dynamic woman.

My exposure to other cultures... makes me a dynamic woman.

My world travels... make me a dynamic woman.

My love for humanity...makes me a dynamic woman.

I think my rich childhood is a continuous gift that gave me purpose. I knew very early on in life that I would work with humanity.

Today I'm a Global Transformational Life Coach helping humanity to heal and experience a life of joy.

"Mèsi Ayiti mwen toujou fou pou ou"

Thank you Haiti! I'm still crazy about you!

Love,

Danita

Danita Sajous has committed her time on this planet to help humans live lives of FUN, FREEDOM and FABULOUSNESS. She has spent over 10 years honing her craft as a Neuro-Transformational Life Coach, Hypnotherapist, Speaker and Retreat Facilitator. p

She has taught, trained and impacted thousands of clients around the globe, and has co-created with some of the top renowned coaches in all of personal development.

Danita's coaching approach stems from an understanding of the subconscious mind, helping her clients break free from the internal challenges and feedback loops that keep most people living a life of mediocrity.

She has helped clients overcome life-long patterns of anxiety, depression and addiction. She helps people dissolve fears of abandonment, rejection and judgment and reconnect to their self-esteem, confidence and joy.

Most importantly, Danita has remained a student of the work, constantly seeking to improve herself daily.

To contact Danita, please see below:

IG: @danitasajous

FB: realtalkwithdanita

website: danitasajous.com

email: danita@danitasajous.com

Chapter 18

The Power of Love
By Margaret Packer

I 'm inspired to acknowledge my truth and share it with you. I was born an illegitimate child to a 37-year-old mother and an absentee father. My mother has three children from three different fathers. I am the youngest of three—two girls and a boy. I'm grateful for the love of my sister who is 13 years my senior and my anchor in the family. She provided me with friendship, made my life easier, and assured me that I wasn't alone.

My sister taught me to say "Black Power" and to understand that it meant security and self-sufficiency. I am also grateful to my brother who is 18 years older than me and loved me unconditionally. I felt this love when he told me he refused to allow his father to call me a "nigger," while simultaneously telling him to get out of his house. His father later apologized to my brother and never repeated that behavior again.

My father was a doctor, yet I grew up only knowing his name. While I'm grateful, it still hurts knowing that he had children from another relationship whom he acknowledged—yet he ignored me. In fact, from my father's side, I have twin sisters who are attorneys and a brother—a doctor, who followed in his footsteps. My father's absence made me feel I wasn't good enough to be called his child. This belief was confirmed when I asked my mother about him and her response was to slap me across my cheek. Her action inflicted not only a physical blow, but also an undeniable emotional pain that lingered in my heart for most of my life. Today, I share this truth as a gateway to a better understanding of my relationship with my mother.

In my younger years, I didn't believe my mother was my biological mom. Her Native-American heritage gave her a warm skin tone—her hair had to be permed to become curly like mine. Some would say she was white-complected with European attributes. She was from South Dakota, growing up on the Reservation.

On the other hand, I am melanin and I look black—of mixed descent. I took the Ancestry test so I could see all of what makes me, me. Upon reflection, I feel proud that as a child, when people asked me about my heritage my patent response ALWAYS reflected BOTH— Not just Native American or Black, but BOTH.

As a child, I was happy to go to the Native American Indian classes my mom held for Native children. I also, distinctly remember being in third grade at Park School and participating in an event—a Native American dance. I wore a Native Dance Shawl with fringed edges and ribbons—and hair braided in two. In my mind, I was Native and thought I could dance, even if I was not in sync with the others. Now I realize: that I was holding onto all I knew as a child.

I am also proud to be African American! My mom was not well educated: I was there when she received her GED. I remember her expression of joy, and the pride I felt about her accomplishment. Despite this lack of education and support from my father, my mother demonstrated her love for me by showing me the importance of BOTH sides of my heritage. She expressed this by taking me to a soul food restaurant and a multi-racial church. I am grateful for those occasions. At the time, as a child, I didn't understand her intentions, but I can see today that my mother was trying to give me roots: African American people and food were the best mechanisms for teaching culture. My mother also enjoyed returning to the Reservation to see her family and making donations of clothing to families in need. I would often take these trips with her, but when I was 14 I no longer wanted to accompany her. The truth is, The Reservation didn't have fast-food restaurants, and quite honestly I felt like some of the Native people didn't like Black people. They didn't feel like family to me, so that's why I went to live with my grandparents who were living only a block away from my mother. My mom continued to remind me that she was still my mother.

During my junior year in high school, I asked my mother if I could live with my sister, seeing that her husband was out of the country. Her response was, "No." —her typical answer to me. That hurt me to the core and I couldn't understand why. I ended up moving to California two days after my high school graduation and I've been living in California ever since.

Before I had my first child I wrote my mother a 13-page letter front and back letting her know that I didn't appreciate what she told me as a child about my father. She said that he was a womanizer and that he did drugs. That didn't feel good because I couldn't understand why she was with him.

For years I paid for my mom to visit me in California. She was happy being with me and so was I. While I loved her, I continued to deal with intense hurt in our relationship. One year when my mom was visiting, my friends Donald and Julie came and were great companions for her. While I loved her I was dealing with so much hurt in our relationship. I felt blessed that my friends were with us, and so we took an excursion to see Kenneth Copeland, Creflo Dollar, and Jesse DuPlantis. They helped me bridge the gap between us—my mother and me. That trip clarified everything: I KNEW I loved my mother, but I just had a hard time letting everything go— the emotional pain.

Another friend, Randy, and I took a trip to Los Angeles and while we were on a train he asked me about my mother. I am pretty sure he was surprised when I expressed my true feelings. He admonished me to NEVER speak those words about my mother again. His words were the most powerful anyone had ever spoken to me. Since that train ride, I only talk about my mother in a way that helps people understand how we've gotten closer.

It finally took a while for me to truly open up to my mom. Because I did not have a close relationship with my mother, I had a yearning for one. I decided to expose all the things I thought about as a child and as an adult and I'm grateful that I did. It took years for our relationship to heal but I am thankful that we have a great relationship today. I made a decision about 14 years ago that if I wanted to have a relationship with my mom I would call her every day. My calls may not be long, however, it's a touch I'm proud to have. She brags about me calling and that makes me happy. We pretty much talk daily and it's a lovely call because she loves me and I love her.

I continually give mom a trip to California. She's happy when she's here; and when she's happy, I'm happy.

I was in my 40s and a mother myself when I recognized why my mom wasn't in many of the pictures that were in my collection. I realized that it was because she was the one taking the pictures! The thought of her taking pictures of me allowed me to see that my mom really loved me. I know this because I took pictures of my children, so they could see all the love that was there for them. I did the same as my mother did and that makes me proud. Though it has taken years, I now cherish our relationship today—my mom and I.

I have recognized that love looks different in every step of my life, so I need to keep on loving myself and keep the door open for loving others—just like I want to be loved. My lesson to you is to be open to love in each phase of your life. **Love is what has transformed me and caused me to be a dynamic woman.**

To become a dynamic woman I had to:

- Forgive myself for the things I thought as a child that was holding me back.
- Forgive others—for myself, so I can live a healthy life.
- Love myself: I took a class to help me see my worth.
- Love others: it's the best thing I can do for them and myself.

Margaret Packer is a daughter, wife, mother, grandmother, International speaker, and consultant. She has traveled the world and love going to jazz concerts and plays. Today she loves who she is and where she's going.

For further information or to contact Margaret see below:

Instagram: @thechocolatepearl

Facebook: Margaret Packer

Email: MrsPacker2010@gmail.com